MW01294478

Healing is by Grace Alone

Dee Henderson

© copyright 2017 by Dee Henderson.

All rights reserved. No part of this publication may be reproduced, stored in retrieval system, or transmitted in any form or by any means – for example, electronic, photocopy, recording – without the express written permission of the publisher. The fair use exception: up to 500 words may be inserted into any publication as long as they are quoted as written and the author and title are indicated as their source.

Contact the author/publisher:
Dee Henderson
P.O. Box 13086
Springfield, IL 62791
dee@deehenderson.com
www.deehenderson.com

current printing revision date: December 16, 2017

Unless otherwise indicated, scripture quotations are from the Revised Standard Version of the Bible, copyright © 1946, 1952, and 1971 National Council of the Churches of Christ in the United States of America. Used by permission. All rights reserved worldwide.

NLT: Scripture quotations marked NLT are taken from the Holy Bible, New Living Translation, copyright ©1996, 2004, 2007, 2013, 2015 by Tyndale House Foundation. Used by permission of Tyndale House Publishers, Inc., Carol Stream, Illinois 60188. All rights reserved.

NIV: Scripture quotations marked NIV are from THE HOLY BIBLE, NEW INTERNATIONAL VERSION®, NIV® Copyright © 1973, 1978, 1984, 2011 by Biblica, Inc.™ Used by permission. All rights reserved worldwide.

KJV: Scripture quotations marked KJV are from the King James Version of The Holy Bible.

Healing Is By Grace Alone

Introduction

Do you want to be well? Do you know someone who needs healed? What does God say about the topic? Those are common needs and questions Christians bring to God.

Jesus healed everyone who came to him of every disease. So a good place to start looking for answers is right there, with Jesus. The apostle John, in his biography about Jesus, begins by describing Jesus this way:

In the beginning was the Word, and the Word was with God, and the Word was God. And the Word became flesh and dwelt among us, full of grace and truth; we have beheld his glory, glory as of the only Son from the Father. (John 1:1,14)

Jesus came to us full of grace and truth. Jesus preached the good news that the kingdom of God was at hand, then showed people what the kingdom of God looks like by his works, and then further explained in a series of parables how the Kingdom of God operates.

I have a special affinity for Jesus' use of telling stories to convey truths he wanted to share. I'm known for the fiction I write, having authored twenty-two novels now. I mostly write fiction because I can tell the heart of something better in a story format.

My most recent manuscript had the subject topic of healing. In it I'm presenting scriptures, talking about them, and telling a story of those scriptures in action. The conclusions I found for the questions I was asking God about the topic of healing surprised me, and at times stunned me. The scriptures show healing is by grace alone, and it comes to us through communion. (And I think raising the dead is the simplest prayer there is.)

"Jesus has forgiven and healed every person in the world. He's done it at the cross for the whole world in advance. It's a free gift of his grace. 1 Peter 2:24 says two things happened on that Friday. 'He himself bore our sins in his body on the tree' and 'By his wounds you have been healed.' Both are past tense statements. Both are inclusive of all of mankind. The Greek word translated wounds is literally the stripe of scourging."

Healing doesn't come to us by our works. Healing is by grace alone. It is a gift from Jesus. That is a life-changing truth to see.

This book is offered with the deep desire that the church would return to enjoying the full five benefits God has for his people, gifts that come from his grace alone.

> Bless the LORD, O my soul;
> and all that is within me, bless his holy name!
> Bless the LORD, O my soul,
> and forget not all his benefits,
> who forgives all your iniquity,
> who heals all your diseases,
> who redeems your life from the Pit,
> who crowns you with steadfast love and mercy,
> who satisfies you with good as long as you live
> so that your youth is renewed like the eagle's.
> (Psalms 103:1-5)

There are approximately 550 scriptures in this book, counting full quotes and references. I am sharing scriptures primarily from the Revised Standard Version translation of the bible, as that has been the one I've carried since high school and from which I have recorded the most study notes. The scriptures quoted from the NIV and NLT and KJV translations are indicated.

I am a practical learner, I like to go to the source and read it for myself. I find biblehub.com useful for reading verses in many translations and as a resource to then look at the underlying Greek or Hebrew original text. Scripture study is actually the easiest adventure we can take, for the Holy Spirit, the one who wrote the scriptures, is with you as your personal teacher. When I read a verse I don't understand, my favorite words are: "I don't understand this. Would you explain it to me, God?" The Holy Spirit never fails to do so with joy; for he loves to teach.

Many of you will read this book because you are searching for what the bible has to say about healing and you are asking God to help you understand the topic. Others of you may be asked what you think about the conclusions in the fiction title, or desire to see how they were reached. So that you don't get obligated to read the full book (Dee Henderson / An Unfinished Death) to figure out what you think, or how to handle questions if they are asked, I'm offering a middle ground, which is this non-fiction book you hold in your hands.

Connie August is a combat medic who has experienced healings and miracles on the battlefield similar to those in scripture. Ryan Cooper is the CEO of a religious-affiliated private hospital. He wants to understand what she has experienced. She wants him to give a chaplain friend a job when he retires from the service. They start a series of conversations which form the core of the story.

Healing is by Grace Alone includes excerpts from many of their conversations and all the related scriptures the book conclusions rest upon. I suggest reading the first 50 pages (the first third), if the topics are helpful and useful, read to page 100 (the second third). If it is still helpful, finish it.

Jesus is beautiful in everything he does. And he is *for us*, completely, with everything we need. Healing and health are his free gifts to us. Come with me and see.

When you're finished with this study, I welcome your comments on what you have read. You can reach me at:

dee@deehenderson.com
www.deehenderson.com

Dee Henderson
P.O. Box 13086
Springfield, IL 62791

Healing Is By Grace Alone

Bible Study

Thank you for taking this journey with me to explore the scriptures. The topics covered in this study include conversations about:

- God's five benefits to you as a believer
- I AM the Lord your Healer
- What we say happens – the prayer of authority
- Jesus at the cross – the atonement – is the source of our forgiveness and our healing
- Communion is God's method for providing healing and life to a believer
- Faith – what it is and how it arrives
- How to raise the dead
- How to heal the sick
- Healing is by grace alone

There are approximately 550 scriptures in this book, counting full quotes and references. I'm teaching through the scriptures in a dialog format, as it is the most instructive way I know to present a truth.

Connie August is a combat medic who has experienced healings and miracles on the battlefield similar to those in scripture. Ryan Cooper is the CEO of a religious-affiliated private hospital. He wants to understand what she has experienced. In this study, you will be listening in as Connie and Ryan have a series of conversations on various topics.

Think of this as an interactive bible study, following along in conversational format with Ryan and his study of the scriptures.

The following select excerpts are presented in the same order as they appear in the book *An Unfinished Death* by Dee Henderson. The included chapter numbers reflect where the excerpts are found within the full book.

Let's begin the journey as Connie and Ryan do, with a good cup of coffee and a conversation about God.

****

3

Ryan arrived at the coffee shop at 7:40 a.m. Monday, loath to be the one who was late. Connie entered at 7:44, waited through the short line and asked for her usual. She joined him with a smile. "So you took me up on the offer."

He held up his own coffee. "Alert and ready, teach."

She laughed at his reply. He held the door for her and they stepped outside. Connie tucked her scarf tighter around her jacket collar and took a long drink of her coffee. "It's cold. Let's move briskly."

Ryan agreed with both remarks and set a pace that would warm them up with the exercise. They headed toward the hospital. She glanced over with surprise as he held out his phone angled to her.

"I'm recording the conversations," he explained, "audio only, since the video would just jump around. I don't want to ask you to repeat something you've already told me—you would find that annoying—and this way I can share the conversations with people later when I'm trying to explain something you said. They can hear it in your own words."

"Thinking ahead, I admire your confidence. I just hope your hand doesn't freeze and you drop that expensive phone."

He laughed. "I'm good, I promise."

"I can't take you where you want to go, Ryan, without teaching you how to get there. So we'll call this lesson one. Let's start with scripture.

> Bless the LORD, O my soul;
> and all that is within me, bless his holy name!
> Bless the LORD, O my soul,
> and forget not all his benefits

"Where am I quoting from? Do you know?"

"I don't know the passage. It sounds like the Psalms," Ryan replied.

She nodded. "I'm quoting Psalm 103. This is a Psalm of David. There are three things it's helpful to remember about David: He is the anointed King of Israel, the Holy Spirit rests upon him and the New Testament calls him a Prophet. There is no one similar to David in the bible for the prominence God gives him as the example for who Jesus will be. Jesus is referred to as the Son of David, one who sits on the throne of David. God calls David a man after his own heart; Jesus is God's 'beloved son with whom I am well pleased.'

"David is not just speaking to the nation of Israel in this Psalm. God is using David to speak to all his people across all the ages: to the Jews under the first covenant of the law and to both the Jews and Gentiles under the second covenant which ushered in the church. This Psalm describes what God will do through Jesus. God fulfilled bringing us these benefits through Jesus. Listen to the opening verses:

> Bless the LORD, O my soul;
> and all that is within me, bless his holy name!
> Bless the LORD, O my soul,
> and forget not all his benefits,
> who forgives all your iniquity,
> who heals all your diseases,
> who redeems your life from the Pit,

who crowns you with steadfast love and mercy,
who satisfies you with good as long as you live
so that your youth is renewed like the eagle's.
(Psalms 103:1-5)

Connie paused a moment to let him reflect on the verses, then said, "Bless the Lord O my soul and forget not all his benefits. How many Christians can name them? How many Christians understand, trust and believe those are God's benefits to them? Listen to the list again:

who forgives all your iniquity,
who heals all your diseases,
who redeems your life from the Pit,
who crowns you with steadfast love and mercy,
who satisfies you with good as long as you live
so that your youth is renewed like the eagle's.

Connie went quiet so he could think about what she had said. Until she had quoted the passage, he couldn't remember hearing it before, though he knew he had read through all the Psalms more than once in his life. He shifted his phone just enough to flip open the bible app and find the passage, read it again and pinned it for quick reference.

"Are you healed right now Ryan?"

He took a moment trying to figure out how to truthfully answer her question in light of his last physical. After about five seconds she simply reached over and patted his jacket sleeve. "How can you successfully ask God to give a gift of healing to someone else when you aren't even sure he has given it to you?"

Connie's words were a lighter punch than last Friday's comment, but they connected. He had to offer a rueful smile. "Point made."

"I'll let you redeem yourself. Answer me these questions. According to Psalm 103, who forgives everything you have ever done wrong?"

"God."

"Who heals you?"

"God."

"Who redeems your life?"

"God."

"Who crowns you with steadfast love and mercy?"

"God."

"Who satisfies you with good always?"

"God."

"What's your part in having those benefits?"

He tried to carefully answer. "Not forgetting them. Knowing they are my benefits. Wanting them. Accepting them."

Connie nodded. "Good answer. Not a single one of those benefits comes because of your own works."

She gave him time to think about it as she finished her coffee, then remarked, "God gives really spectacular free gifts. It would be good if we knew what they were. We perish for lack of knowledge. Lack of knowledge of God's word and faith in God's word. We basically don't trust the God who wrote those words. We can't list his benefits. We don't believe them when we hear them. And then we wonder why we struggle as Christians."

She glanced over to kindly smile at him. "You really want lesson two?"

He laughed. "I admit, I'm going to feel like a piece of swiss cheese by the time you get done skewering me with truth, taking me through what you know, but I'm not walking in this cold because I want the easy teacher who grades on a curve. What's lesson two?"

"You are a brave man. Exodus 15:26b. 'I am the LORD, your healer.' We'll get to it tomorrow."

The hospital was up ahead. They were about to part ways. He reluctantly shut off the recording. "Thanks, Connie. This was very helpful."

"If you show up for coffee tomorrow, you can expect to be asked what your five benefits are."

"Homework. And you say you're not a teacher."

She laughed. "Goodbye, Ryan."

She turned away from the hospital in the direction of her pizza shop. Half a block away, she turned. "Hey, Ryan." He slipped off the earpiece, having started the conversation playing back so he could go through it again. "What's that way?" She pointed west toward the other buildings in the hospital complex.

"Beyond the clinic buildings, mostly parking lots and the hospital rehab center, the garden park." The clinic buildings where doctors saw patients were hospital owned but mostly leased out to physician groups.

Connie looked at her phone judging the time. "Give me six more minutes and let's circle as far as the garden park. I'm getting nudged pretty hard to say one more thing."

"Sure."

He walked back to join her and set a new recording to start. He led the way toward the garden park and, conscious of the time limit, didn't interrupt to ask what she meant by that nudge remark, filing it away to ask later.

Connie began with a comment. "There's a scripture in Hebrews that is a warning the Holy Spirit directed Paul to write to believers:

Take care, brethren, lest there be in any of you an evil, unbelieving heart, leading you to fall away from the living God. But exhort one another every day, as long as it is called "today," that none of you may be hardened by the deceitfulness of sin. For we share in Christ, if only we hold our first confidence firm to the end, (Hebrews 3:12-14)

Connie gestured with her coffee. "I need to offer an important comment about God. He's righteous and he's made us righteous like him. We hear that word, but it often goes by as a concept and doesn't always sink in. I'd like to make it practical. Listen to these attributes of God.

This is the message we have heard from him and proclaim to you, that God is light and in him is no darkness at all. (1 John 1:5)

Every good endowment and every perfect gift is from above, coming down from the Father of lights with whom there is no variation or shadow due to change. Of his own will he brought us forth by the word of truth that we should be a kind of first fruits of his creatures. (James 1:17-18)

God is not man, that he should lie,
or a son of man, that he should repent.
Has he said and will he not do it?
Or has he spoken and will he not fulfil it?
(Numbers 23:19)

And the word of the LORD came to me, saying, "Jeremiah, what do you see?" And I said, "I see a rod of almond." Then the LORD said to me, "You have seen well, for I am watching over my word to perform it." (Jeremiah 1:11-12)

"That last one is a play on words; the Hebrew words for almonds and watching are a single letter apart. God was giving Jeremiah a visual way to remember his point," Connie explained.

"That's God, as the Holy Spirit Himself would have us see Him. God is light. God keeps his word, He performs it. God does not lie. I like how God's interactions with us illustrate that. Listen to what a verse says about his relationship with Sarah.

The LORD visited Sarah as he had said and the LORD did to Sarah as he had promised. (Genesis 21:1)

"God is faithful, he keeps his word, he does not lie," Connie stressed.

"Got it," Ryan replied.

She smiled. "Do you? Because God equips us to be the same—to be faithful, to keep our word, to not lie. He's made us righteous like himself." She paused and then shifted the conversation the other direction. "Now I want you to switch from thinking about God and righteousness, to the devil and evil.

He [the devil] was a murderer from the beginning and has nothing to do with the truth, because there is no truth in him. When he lies, he speaks according to his own nature, for he is a liar and the father of lies. (John 8:44b)

The thief [satan] comes only to steal and kill and destroy (John 10:10a)

The reason the Son of God appeared was to destroy the works of the devil. (1 John 3:8b)

"See clearly the difference between God and satan?" Connie asked.

Ryan had to smile at the question she had set him up to answer. "I do."

Connie nodded. "Good. Then let me make a very serious point: one of the deepest errors we can ever make in our Christian walk is to think God isn't telling us the truth. Don't ever offend God by thinking he is like satan. God does not lie. We can have questions, wonder about things and need help from God to figure out our experience in the light of the scripture; that's growing up in Christ. But saying something God wrote in his word isn't true is to call God a liar. We are so painfully wrong in our thinking about our God at times that we have to be reminded of the most basic fact that God does not lie."

Ryan registered her point and more seriously nodded.

Connie thought for a moment then added, "It helps if we see the picture of just how stark the difference is between God and satan. For one thing satan is not God's equal, satan is a created being, an angel; whose parallel would be the angel Gabriel or the angel Michael. Satan is not all knowing, not all powerful, not able to be everywhere at the same time. God is all those things.

"Satan went from being an angel of light standing in God's presence leading worship, one of the three chief angels, one of the most beautiful beings in all God's creation, to stumbling, letting in pride and scripture says iniquity was found in him. God hurled Lucifer out of his presence and changed his name to satan. Satan's sin was to want the worship that was due only to God. That pride has consumed satan. All that was beautiful in him has turned to only darkness as he's now outside of God's presence, outside of God's light.

"A man, consumed by sin and evil thoughts, dies and his evil dies with him. Our darkness is limited to what accumulates in a lifetime. Satan never dies. There has been no end to his ever-increasing darkness. Satan has thoroughly become the evil one. The angels who fell with him have become demons as they too now live outside the light of God. At the last judgment, satan and the demons will be cast in the lake of fire for eternity to remove their evil from creation.

"Man thinks a little darkness is no big deal, we all have sinned; God's grace will cover us. And His grace will, but it is designed to pull us out of that sin and darkness spiral, not to make us comfortable with some darkness left in us because we're too lazy to renew our minds and put on Christ. God calls us to be children of light.

"We listen to God's word, but do not hear the truth, when our hearts have grown hard. The truth doesn't register with us. What God is saying, it doesn't sink in. That's the warning the Holy Spirit had Paul write. Don't harden your heart. Guard against doubt. Questions are fine and good and how the Lord teaches wisdom. Admitting you don't understand something is a humble move which lets God guide and teach you from that point to find and understand the truth. But to close the door to the word of God with a thought 'that's not true' can be one of the most devastating self-inflicted injuries you can do to yourself.

"God is righteous, a God in whom there is no darkness. Don't ever offend God by attributing to him the darkness which is in satan. Satan is a liar. God is not. What God has written in his word is true.

> Bless the LORD, O my soul;
> and all that is within me, bless his holy name!
> Bless the LORD, O my soul,
> and forget not all his benefits,
> who forgives all your iniquity,
> who heals all your diseases,
> who redeems your life from the Pit,
> who crowns you with steadfast love and mercy,
> who satisfies you with good as long as you live
> so that your youth is renewed like the eagle's.
> (Psalms 103:1-5)

"And with that, I'm two minutes past my stretched time and going to have to move like lightning. Sorry," Connie said, already moving away.

"Go," Ryan urged.

She tossed her empty coffee cup in a trash barrel and set out at a comfortable run toward her shop. Ryan watched the grace of her movements. She'd spent years running, that stride wasn't a self-conscious woman trying to run for exercise. Combat medic. He reminded himself with the title just what her life had been like for eight years.

Ryan realized he hadn't shut off the recording and did so, glad he had that extra eight minutes recorded.

He turned back to the main hospital building and wondered aloud, "God, how many times recently have I just assumed the reason my experience wasn't yielding results was because you were speaking in a generalized way? I'd read that 'the prayer of faith will save the sick man' and mentally add on the word 'sometimes', never facing the fact I was calling you a liar by doing so. My head and my heart hurt right now and that was only about 25 minutes with her. Forgive me, God, sincerely, for not believing your word means what it says. I asked what the problem was and you just held up a mirror to show me part of the problem is me."

The Holy Spirit had sliced clean, Ryan was grateful for that. Delivered the blow but not pressed on the weight of the guilt after his eyes opened. Ryan slipped in the earpiece and replayed Connie's words as he turned toward the hospital main building to listen to it again, using his bible app as he walked to locate the scriptures she had quoted.

He'd be wise to start some study notes for these conversations as they were going to be rich in verses if this one was typical. She wasn't just quoting scripture, her statements themselves were often referencing scripture. These were going to be very useful walks.

****

Ryan Notes / conversation one / additional references

My people are destroyed for lack of knowledge (Hosea 4:6a)

Now war arose in heaven, Michael and his angels fighting against the dragon; and the dragon and his angels fought, but they were defeated and there was no longer any place for them in heaven. And the great dragon was thrown down, that ancient serpent, who is called the Devil and Satan, the deceiver of the whole world -- he was thrown down to the earth and his angels were thrown down with him. And I heard a loud voice in heaven, saying, "Now the salvation and the power and the kingdom of our God and the authority of his Christ have come, for the accuser of our brethren has been thrown down, who accuses them day and night before our God. And they have conquered him by the blood of the Lamb and by the word of their testimony, for they loved not their lives even unto death. Rejoice then, O heaven and you that dwell therein! But woe to you, O earth and sea, for the devil has come down to you in great wrath, because he knows that his time is short!" (Revelation 12:7-12)

He who commits sin is of the devil; for the devil has sinned from the beginning. (1 John 3:8a)

4

Tuesday morning Connie walked into the coffee shop at 7:45 a.m. and Ryan simply said "Connie" and nodded to his table. He'd remembered her standing order and bought it for her before she arrived to save her the time in line.

She accepted with a grateful smile, took a first sip of the coffee and let him hold the door. "I wasn't sure you would show after round one with me."

He smiled. "What can I say, I'm a man who knows what's good for me can occasionally sting. I can take hearing truth, even when it's personally convicting." He made an observation, wondering how she'd take the personal remark. "You look particularly tired, Connie," he mentioned, concerned.

"A long night," she replied, "which makes the coffee even more appreciated." She didn't explain further. She nodded to his phone. "You'll need the recording today, this lesson has branches. Exodus 15:26b. 'I am the LORD, your healer.' How many names does God give himself?"

She went straight to the topic of the day and he switched to follow her, glad he knew this answer. "Seven. I AM the Lord who sees you. I AM the Lord who provides. I AM the Lord your victory, something like that. The other three escape me."

She nodded. "In Hebrew the names were like hyphenated words, they weren't such a mouthful as the English translations. They're like us saying one of our titles is CPA, Doctor, Pilot, Lawyer. The title is a statement of our training and skill, what you can expect us to be an expert at doing. God's names are self-given statements about himself. Unlike how we would say 'I am a writer', or 'I am a doctor' and it is part of who we are, but not the whole of us, God's names are more like facets of his being, a deeper statement of who he is all the way through. And God says one of his names is 'I AM the Lord your Healer.'"

She ate part of the sweet roll with obvious pleasure before she continued, nodding her thanks for that breakfast. "God tells his people that name at the time of the Exodus. They've left Egypt and are heading across the wilderness to the promised land. God is ready to pile on them good gifts, to give them, in his own words, 'great and goodly cities, which you did not build and houses full of all good things, which you did not fill and cisterns hewn out, which you did not hew and vineyards and olive trees, which you did not plant' (Deuteronomy 6:10b,11a) It's a pretty cool list. That's our God, how he thinks when he says 'I'm going to bless you.' We underestimate today what God's idea of being good to his people looks like. Anyway. Even before Israel gets to that promised land, God has started blessing them by announcing this one of his seven names."

She glanced at him, curious. "Why do we think we have to talk God into healing people? He likes healing people. God basically hung out a shingle that said, 'I'm your doctor, appointments are free' and wanted anyone who got sick to come see him.

"And where did we get the idea that God stopped being himself?" Connie asked with wonder. "God didn't change his name after a hundred years and say, 'I've had enough of this, no one comes and I don't really like healing people anymore anyway.' No, the Father says about himself in the Old Testament book of Malachi 'I the LORD do not change' It's Malachi 3:6a. He's always been a God who defines himself as 'I AM the Lord your Healer.'"

Connie drank more of her coffee and Ryan chose not to interrupt with a comment, as time on this walk was all too brief.

"David was King of Israel around roughly 1,000 B.C.," Connie mentioned. "So the Exodus goes back to something like 1,500 B.C. One thousand five hundred years after God says 'I AM the Lord your Healer', Jesus shows up and heals every person who comes to him of *every* disease and says 'I'm only doing my Father's will'. That's a pretty amazing picture. God the Father clearly hadn't changed his name in over fifteen hundred years.

"Jesus healed people because the power of the Holy Spirit rested upon him. The Holy Spirit is God. And God likes to heal, its one of his self-given names. After the resurrection, Jesus returns to heaven and the Holy Spirit arrives more broadly on earth with the birth of the church. He's here to dwell with us and be in us, those who believe in Jesus, forever. Now what do you think the Holy Spirit would like to do for you and me and everyone around us? Heal us. The Holy Spirit with us today is the exactly same Holy Spirit which descended from heaven and remained on Jesus. And right now he's walking around earth with us marveling at all the sick people we simply let walk past."

Connie paused their conversation and Ryan realized she was studying the people coming their direction, taking to heart her own words. She let ten people walk by, then quietly said, "Headaches, flu, back pain. And we walk right by without offering help in Jesus' name."

She shifted from that remark back to her topic without explaining further and Ryan nearly interrupted. He needed more time with her than these brief walks were giving him, because he heard the confidence in her remark that she could in fact help those passing by be healed. He was so incredibly hungry to understand how to do just that.

"God is a triune God, three persons who are one," Connie continued. "God the Father, God the Son, Jesus our

Savior and God the Holy Spirit. God is three persons and yet one, the trinity. In the New Testament, the Holy Spirit is also called the Spirit of God, the Spirit of Jesus and the Spirit of Grace. Think of the Holy Spirit as the innermost part of God. If you want to know God's heart, just look at what the Holy Spirit is doing. And scripture says it's by the Holy Spirit we are being healing today.

If the Spirit of him who raised Jesus from the dead dwells in you, he who raised Christ Jesus from the dead will give life to your mortal bodies also through his Spirit which dwells in you. (Romans 8:11)

"God likes to heal. If he didn't, he would have said so. Instead, he made healing one of his very names. We need to get a clear look at that truth and let it plant itself firmly in our hearts. The Father doesn't change. He never will. And Jesus, who is the image of the Father, doesn't change. He never will, either. Hebrews 13:8 says 'Jesus Christ is the same yesterday and today and for ever.'"

Her phone rang and she ignored it. They were almost at the hospital. "God encourages us to get to know him, to realize that because there's no variation of change in Him, we can trust what we learn to always be true. God is reassuring us that every little bit we figure out about Him is going to be true forever. God likes to heal people. He will like to heal people for all eternity. That's the lesson for today.

"We do not have to convince God to heal someone. He's been the God who wants to heal us for the last three thousand five hundred years, ever since he announced His name to us. He hasn't changed in his willingness or desire or power to do so. The problem the church is dealing with is not with God. It's in us."

****

Ryan located related scriptures as he listened to the audio again that night, adding them to the notes he was making.

Ryan Notes / conversation two / additional references

The seven names God gives himself
God is our Righteousness
God is our Peace
God is our Guide / Shepherd
God is our Physician / Healer
God is our Provider / Source
God is Ever Present
God is our Victory

On the last day of the feast, the great day, Jesus stood up and proclaimed, "If any one thirst, let him come to me and drink. He who believes in me, as the scripture has said, `Out of his heart shall flow rivers of living water.'" Now this he said about the Spirit, which those who believed in him were to receive; for as yet the Spirit had not been given, because Jesus was not yet glorified. (John 7:37-39)

And I will pray the Father and he will give you another Counselor, to be with you for ever, even the Spirit of truth, whom the world cannot receive, because it neither sees him nor knows him; you know him, for he dwells with you and will be in you. (John 14:16-17)

But the Counselor, the Holy Spirit, whom the Father will send in my name, he will teach you all things and bring to your remembrance all that I have said to you. (John 14:26)

When the Spirit of truth comes, he will guide you into all the truth; for he will not speak on his own authority, but whatever he hears he will speak and he will declare to you the things that are to come. He will glorify me, for he will take what is mine and declare it to you. (John 16:13-14)

5

Wednesday morning brought a burst of mild spring weather. Ryan changed his order to an iced coffee to celebrate and shared a snack sack of donut holes with Connie as they walked, doing his best to keep his phone far enough away from the sack so as not to pick up the noise of rustling paper.

"How does God do stuff?" Connie asked. "God is Spirit, he's invisible, he lives in an invisible world called heaven and yet he made the visible one. What does the bible tell us about how God does stuff? How does the invisible affect the visible?"

Ryan offered one verse that came to mind. "In creation, 'God said, "Let there be light"; and there was light.'"

Connie nodded. "Genesis 1:3a." She held out her hand and the sunlight highlighted her skin. She turned her hand and let the light play across her palm. "God speaks and things happen in the visible world. I'm showing you one of the most beautiful examples of that right now. Look at the light landing on my hand. God's first recorded words, 'Let there be light' and I'm basking in his words right now. I can trace the light and the warmth I'm feeling directly to God's first words recorded in Genesis. That is astonishing. And it's a profound truth into understanding what scripture is and how it works. The word of God creates tangible reality in the visible world. We're still enjoying the words He spoke at creation.

"God's words have always had power in them. What God says happens. 'Let there be light'; and there was light. God speaks and what he says comes to pass. One of the keys to understanding God and our relationship with Him is to understand how the invisible and visible are linked by words.

By faith we understand that the world was created by the word of God, so that what is seen was made out of things which do not appear. (Hebrews 11:3)

"Lesson one, God doesn't lie. It's more than a moral statement about God, a statement of his righteousness, though it is that. I actually think it's impossible for God to lie. His words create and do what he's spoken. To lie, God would have to speak a word without power in it. I don't think it's possible for God to speak a word without power in it. God speaks and his words make stuff happen in the visible realm. God speaks and what he says comes to pass.

"Now Jesus comes to earth, sent by the Father. Jesus comes to earth as a man. He has emptied himself, literally set aside his power as God. Jesus is a man with a human nature like ours. Yet Jesus speaks and what he says comes to pass. 'Peace! Be still!' And the wind and waves obey him.

And he [Jesus] awoke and rebuked the wind and said to the sea, "Peace! Be still!" And the wind ceased and there was a great calm. He said to them [his disciples in the boat with him], "Why are you afraid? Have you no faith?" And they were filled with awe and said to one another, "Who then is this, that even wind and sea obey him?" (Mark 4:39-41)

"Jesus is a man, but he's acting a lot like God. His words are impacting the visible world. Material things obey the words of Jesus. Why? How's that possible?"

Ryan didn't try to answer, recognizing Connie was unfolding a thought with the questions.

"Jesus is using words like God uses words, to change the visible world by what he says. Jesus is a man of like nature as us. When he's ordering things around, he's doing so as a man. The key is that Jesus is also the Son of God, a man born of the Holy Spirit, with the Holy Spirit resting upon him. Jesus' words were causing stuff to happen by using the Father's power, by drawing on the family connection. Jesus has the authority the Father has, because he is a son.

"Jesus didn't have to be adopted to be that son. He was God's first-born son. His standing as a son of God was sufficient for the man Jesus to be able to act as God does, for his words to have power, even though Jesus as a man was just as limited as we are.

"Jesus told Peter to 'Come!' and Peter walked on water. Jesus spoke a word of command and in that word was the power of God to do what that word said.

"There are two types of men in the world, walking around on earth. Fallen men, whose words have no power. And born-again men, adopted sons of God, born of the Holy Spirit, whose words have been restored to power. Believers will use words the same way Jesus uses them.

"...For truly, I say to you, if you have faith as a grain of mustard seed, you will say to this mountain, `Move from here to there,' and it will move; and nothing will be impossible to you." (Matthew 17:20b)

"We are the adopted sons of God, we have the Holy Spirit dwelling in us. Jesus is impressing upon us that God will treat us as true sons. Our words will cause things to happen. Just as God's words create and do what He has said, just as Jesus' words create and do what he said, our words will create and do what we say.

"There is a reality to how God does stuff and how a son of God does stuff. And that's our reality now. When Jesus says your words move mountains he is not being figurative. Jesus was showing us how a son of God does stuff. We use our words. 'Nothing will be impossible to you.' Jesus is being literal. Jesus means exactly that, with all the implications those words *nothing* and *impossible* convey. Our words now have power because we are children of God. True sons.

"To understand prayer, you have to realize you are not speaking powerless words that a fallen man might say. You are a true son of God and your words have the power to change the visible world. We have been adopted; we are sons of God. We have authority in our words when they are spoken with faith."

She looked ahead and stopped. They were at the hospital. Yet another morning was ending with a thought of massive substance being offered and she was going to simply leave it there. Ryan wanted the next five sentences, the next five paragraphs, but it wasn't fair to make her late to work. "Thank you Connie." He closed the recording. "I'm looking forward to the rest of this conversation."

****

Ryan arrived at Connie's Pizza at 2:50 p.m. Wednesday, grateful to find the lights were still on and caught motion inside as Connie set chairs up on tables, preparing to mop. He leaned against the brick of the building and waited for her to finish the wrap up.

Jesus, she needs to say yes and I know what I'm asking. Help me. His prayer had the edge of desperation to it, mirroring his thoughts and why he had made the decision to leave the hospital and drive over.

The door opened at 3:05 p.m. Connie stepped out humming a tune and stopped with surprise when she saw him waiting for her.

"I've got a 10-year-old girl dying of cancer. Help me."

Connie studied him for a long minute. She used her key to lock the door. When she turned back to him, she didn't say no, so he took part of his prayer as answered. "My time is particularly packed today Ryan. It's going to need to be no introductions to people, no extra conversations, no lost minutes to other things."

"I can do that," he replied promptly.

"Then let's go." She turned to walk in the direction of the hospital.

"I drove over, Connie." He unlocked his car, grateful he'd been able to find an open spot on her block and held the passenger door for her. "Thanks for this."

"I haven't done anything yet."

"You're coming."

He checked traffic and pulled away from the curb. "Do you want to know any particulars about her history?"

"What's her name and what's her relation to you?"

"Joy Ellen Patterson. Her father is a good friend of a surgeon on staff. I've known the family casually for the ten years since Joy's birth."

"The parent's names?"

"Dan and Amy."

"That's enough to know for now."

He started a recording and set his phone between them. "What you were talking about this morning, our words have power because of the son relationship we now have with God. Tell me more." He was asking her to pray for someone dying of cancer and expecting her to do something about it. He intensely needed to understand what she knew about prayer.

"Ryan."

"I won't hold you to being eloquent about it, just tell me what comes to mind about the topic that you think I should know."

She shifted in her seat to better see him. "We're in a relationship with God now, it's not a piece of paper, a *'young man you should sign a different last name now'* kind of formality. The God who created and rules the universe just adopted us as his sons and daughters. Every being in the invisible world just sat up and took notice. One of the first gifts God gives us is authority of position: we are sons of God. As sons, we now share God's way of operating. We have authority in our words. God gives us the right to have what we say. I can give you the scriptures easier than a lot of words right now. This is not my best time of day.

"...For truly, I say to you, if you have faith as a grain of mustard seed, you will say to this mountain, `Move from here to there,' and it will move; and nothing will be impossible to you." (Matthew 17:20b)

"...And whatever you ask in prayer, you will receive, if you have faith." (Matthew 21:22)

"You want to know what God considers fair game to do with your words, just look at Jesus. He always did the will of the Father. He came as a man, the first-born son of God, he had the Holy Spirit with him. He's using his words to change the visible world. And in particular he's going after sickness and disease. Jesus hates the works of the devil, he came to destroy them and he's doing so using his authority as a son. A good summary is in Matthew:

And he [Jesus] went about all Galilee, teaching in their synagogues and preaching the gospel of the kingdom and healing every disease and every infirmity among the people. (Matthew 4:23)

"When Jesus is healing every disease and every infirmity what he's doing is giving people the reality of what the gospel of the kingdom means, he's showing and giving people what he's just been teaching and preaching. That is his entire ministry, talking about the kingdom and then giving it to people. For example:

Now when John heard in prison about the deeds of the Christ, he sent word by his disciples and said to him, "Are you he who is to come, or shall we look for another?" And Jesus answered them, "Go and tell John what you hear and see: the blind receive their sight and the lame walk, lepers are cleansed and the deaf hear and the dead are raised up and the poor have good news preached to them. And blessed is he who takes no offense at me." (Matthew 11:2-6) they brought him [Jesus] all the sick, those afflicted with various diseases and pains, demoniacs, epileptics and paralytics and he healed them. (Matthew 4:24b)

Connie used her fingers to list the points she wanted him to remember. "Jesus healed everyone of every disease. He's showing people the Father, the one who said I AM the Lord your Healer. He's talking about the kingdom of God and then giving it to us. We're Jesus' disciples. Jesus said in John 20:21a 'As the Father has sent me, even so I send you.' Jesus expects us to be doing what he did, tell people about the kingdom of God and then give it to them.

"A disciple is not above his teacher, nor a servant above his master; it is enough for the disciple to be like his teacher and the servant like his master." (Matthew 10:24-25a)

"Truly, truly, I say to you, he who believes in me will also do the works that I do; and greater works than these will he do, because I go to the Father. Whatever you ask in my name, I will do it, that the Father may be glorified in the Son; if you ask anything in my name, I will do it." (John 14:12-14)

"Those verses from John are wonderfully reassuring—you will also do the works I do—it's a promise we can lean against, we have Jesus' word on it, we will do in Jesus' name what would otherwise be impossible for a man to do. But Christians rarely see what else that verse is. It's actually a warning. If you aren't doing my works, you don't believe me. He said follow me and be like me.

"Jesus would like to remind you of your new title, 'Hey, you're my Ambassadors. It wasn't theory, it's an actual job with works to do. He who believes in me will also do the works I do. Go heal the sick, raise the dead, cast out demons. You are an adopted son of God. The Holy

Spirit is with you. I'm right there, for I will be with you always. Stop watching satan kill, steal and destroy. Act. Give me something to work with. Go stop what the devil is doing.'

"Jesus has decided what he does now on earth he will do through us, so he can teach us how to be who we really are, adopted sons of God. It's like Aaron who spoke for Moses. No one mistook who they each were. I don't heal, God does. He just needs someone to show up with faith and speak from delegated authority so he can do what he desires to do.

"The centurion told Jesus, 'just say the word and my servant will be healed.' He said that because he understood authority. Whatever Jesus said, that is what would be done. Jesus called that confidence—that knowledge of and in, his authority—great faith. We need to trust Jesus' word to us that we now have permission to speak in his name. I know Jesus' authority over disease and death. So I give Jesus something to work with. I trust and know I have authority to speak in his name and I speak with the confidence that what I say in his name is what is going to be done."

Ryan pulled into the parking garage at the hospital and felt again the frustration of not having just one more minute, two more, so she could give him the next paragraph of that thought. He parked near the elevator on the lower level. "Thanks, Connie." He closed the recording. "Joy's in the ICU."

6

After a last check with ICU on Joy's condition— asleep, holding steady—Ryan went home just after nine p.m. knowing he'd be called if she took a turn for the worse. Walter was with the family. He dumped his wallet on the dresser, stepped out of his shoes, tugged the oldest sports shirt from the chest of drawers and with relief hung up the suit.

"God, hope tonight is at war with the reality of a history of cancer losses. Knowing someone who believes in you with great faith has prayed for Joy is why I have hope. Reality is I can give you the names of those in similar situations to Joy who have died. It's good to talk about the subject with Connie. My heart is grabbing hold of her words and hope is springing to life, yet reality is like sand rubbing against my skin. I don't want to speak words of doubt with you tonight, to not anticipate a good outcome, but there is the fact I'm struggling tonight to believe this can turn around, that prayer can do this. Without calling you a liar, or what Connie has explained being wrong—I can feel the truth in how she describes Jesus—I need you to open my eyes to see why I don't have much confidence in you. Is it simply the reality of so many situations similar to tonight that my entire soul has already braced for bad news and doesn't want to let hope get traction? I'm carrying home the reality Joy may die tonight and am bracing for that event. I don't want to take it anymore, God. I'd rather go shovel snow in Alaska than deal with more kids dying on me. You can take it as given if Joy loses this fight and dies tonight, I'm going to ask Connie to come pray for her before the doctors officially call time of death. Whatever you'd like to say tonight, I'm listening as best I know how."

He got a cold soda from the kitchen and headed into his home office. He'd known when he went to get Connie this afternoon this would be the result. Hope, warring against reality, with him uncertain which way this fulcrum was going to tip tonight. Would he have the guts to brush himself off if Joy didn't make it and go back to listening to what else Connie said without the doubts piling up?

"I didn't intend to put her on trial and implicitly, to put you on trial, God. It's simply the situation that arose. I want to process what happens with wisdom and learn from it. Joy's won't be the first death to cancer where we lost the fight, but it would be the first loss since hope was sitting in my heart with an expectation we could turn things around even this close to death. Jesus, you didn't have failures. That would be a very nice place to reach. I don't want to endure another one. I need to ask Connie how many she has prayed for without seeing the result she asked. I should have let her set my expectations earlier. Connie… she just speaks with such confidence, you know when you're with her it's a sure thing and then the reality begins to flow by and I admit, I'm not standing on rock right now, confident in what's going to happen. Help me, God."

He needed to study, to get his mind back in the scriptures and give the Holy Spirit some room to work. It was the last thing he wanted to do, setting himself up for a steeper fall, but it was the most important thing he had to do. Connie had spent 5 minutes with Joy and left. He didn't think it was because she had looked at the situation, said I can't do anything, said a perfunctory few words and left. She'd come to the hospital because he asked, prayed for Joy and left because she was satisfied she'd done what she came to do. He desperately needed to understand that confidence she had, how it had built in her.

Ryan listened to the day's two audios and he added notes late into the night, relieved as time passed and his phone stayed silent. He dug deep for fresh insights, reading through the gospel of Matthew. Jesus had healed, not as God, but as a man who had the Holy Spirit with him. Jesus had been healing everyone of every disease out of that trust relationship he had with his Father. Doing it as a man, one who was a son of God. Realizing Jesus was modeling what adopted sons of God would also do Connie had fearlessly moved that direction herself. Ryan had been praying for a breakthrough in understanding, when it had been here all along, waiting for him to see it. God had held up a mirror for him to see the problem in himself. Now God was shining a light on the scriptures, helping him see and understand what he had only read before. Connie was basing that confidence of hers on what she found in Jesus' life. It felt good to absorb the words of scripture, even if he was still struggling to grasp their implications. He didn't have that confidence she did yet.

****

Ryan Notes / conversation three / additional references

And he [Jesus] went about all Galilee, teaching in their synagogues and preaching the gospel of the kingdom and healing every disease and every infirmity among the people. (Matthew 4:23)

So his [Jesus] fame spread throughout all Syria and they brought him all the sick, those afflicted with various diseases and pains, demoniacs, epileptics and paralytics and he healed them. (Matthew 4:24)

And when Jesus entered Peter's house, he saw his mother-in-law lying sick with a fever; he touched her hand and the fever left her and she rose and served him. (Matthew 8:14-15)

That evening they brought to him [Jesus] many who were possessed with demons; and he cast out the spirits with a word and healed all who were sick. This was to fulfil what was spoken by the prophet Isaiah, "He took our infirmities and bore our diseases." (Matthew 8:16-17)

When he [Jesus] came down from the mountain, great crowds followed him; and behold, a leper came to him and knelt before him, saying, "Lord, if you will, you can make me clean." And he stretched out his hand and touched him, saying, "I will; be clean." And immediately his leprosy was cleansed. And Jesus said to him, "See that you say nothing to any one; but go, show yourself to the priest and offer the gift that Moses commanded, for a proof to the people." (Matthew 8:1-4)

As he [Jesus] entered Caper'na-um, a centurion came forward to him, beseeching him and saying, "Lord, my servant is lying paralyzed at home, in terrible distress." And he said to him, "I will come and heal him." But the centurion answered him, "Lord, I am not worthy to have you come under my roof; but only say the word and my servant will be healed. For I am a man under authority, with soldiers under me; and I say to one, `Go,' and he goes and to another, `Come,' and he comes and to my slave, `Do this,' and he does it." When Jesus heard him, he marveled and said to those who followed him, "Truly, I say to you, not even in Israel have I found such faith." And to the centurion Jesus said, "Go; be it done for you as you have believed." And the servant was healed at that very moment. (Matthew 8:5-10,13)

And behold, they brought to him a paralytic, lying on his bed; and when Jesus saw their faith he said to the paralytic, "Take heart, my son; your sins are forgiven." And behold, some of the scribes said to themselves, "This man is blaspheming." But Jesus, knowing their thoughts, said, "Why do you think evil in your hearts? For which is easier, to say, `Your sins are forgiven,' or to say, `Rise and walk'? But that you may know that the Son of man has authority on earth to forgive sins" – he then said to the paralytic – "Rise, take up your bed and go home." And he rose and went home. When the crowds saw it, they were afraid and they glorified God, who had given such authority to men. (Matthew 9:2-8)

And behold, a woman who had suffered from a hemorrhage for twelve years came up behind him and touched the fringe of his garment; for she said to herself, "If I only touch his garment, I shall be made well." Jesus turned and seeing her he said, "Take heart, daughter; your faith has made you well." And instantly the woman was made well. (Matthew 9:20-22)

And Jesus went on from there and passed along the Sea of Galilee. And he went up on the mountain and sat down there. And great crowds came to him, bringing with them the lame, the maimed, the blind, the dumb and many others and they put them at his feet and he healed them, so that the throng wondered, when they saw the dumb speaking, the maimed whole, the lame walking and the blind seeing; and they glorified the God of Israel. (Matthew 15:29-31)

And when they had crossed over, they came to land at Gennesaret. And when the men of that place recognized him [Jesus], they sent round to all that region and brought to him all that were sick and besought him that they might only touch the fringe of his garment; and as many as touched it were made well. (Matthew 14:34-36)

And the blind and the lame came to him [Jesus] in the temple and he healed them. (Matthew 21:14)

7

Ryan was waiting outside the coffee shop Thursday, holding a carry container with their coffees and a sack with breakfast, as Connie approached. "I tipped Linda an extra dollar and said you'd see her tomorrow," he mentioned, eager to share his good news. "Joy's sleeping comfortably. Her vitals are good. They took her off the ventilator this morning. She's breathing comfortably on her own."

Connie simply smiled and took the coffee and breakfast he offered. "Good."

"You expected this."

"Of course. God does excellent work. I actually don't think he can do sloppy work, it would violate his perfection. There are all kinds of things God can't do: God can't lie; God can't do sloppy work; God can't not love us, for he *is* love and his steadfast love will continue forever."

Ryan smiled at the way she said it. "Thank you for helping her. It's a big deal, seeing this improvement. Teach me the rest of it, Connie, what you did and how." He knew he was in the early hours of watching a miracle unfold and the one who had brought it had needed only five minutes.

"It's not complicated, Ryan. Jesus heals because it is the just thing to do. Having taken our sins, death has no more claim on us. Jesus heals to restore justice.

"Of all the reasons God could heal us—he loves us, he's our creator, he enjoys being merciful—the reason scripture says he heals us is because Jesus' shed blood has forgiven all our sins and not just ours, but the sins of the whole world. Death which followed sin into the world has no claim, no legal right, to touch us anymore. Sickness and disease are simply the visible signs death is beginning to destroy life. And our God is a righteous judge.

"When we rebelled and sinned, satan had rights, because we gave them to him. Jesus paid the penalty for that sin, crushed satan and freed us, so there's no legal claim death can make against us anymore. With God, healing is a matter of justice, as much as it is a matter of compassion and love. Death is touching this person and he has no legal right to do so." She shrugged. "So it's… 'In Jesus' name, death, get your hands off Joy.' He does. He doesn't have a choice in the matter. The judge has ruled.

"There are different kinds of faith and different kinds of prayers, that's a conversation of its own, but faith when it comes to healing is, at its core, knowing the ground you stand on. You can heal anyone in the world by knowing what the righteous judge has already ruled on the matter. Amen is 'so be it', it's the judge's hammer coming down, enforcing the matter. Jesus heals people because he has dealt with sin. You bring the healing by speaking that verdict in his name."

It was a bigger answer than Ryan had expected to hear, so big it was astonishing. She gave him a moment and smiled. "Listen to the scriptures, you'll see it:

...sin came into the world through one man [Adam] and death through sin (Romans 5:12a)

by one man's disobedience [Adam] many were made sinners, so by one man's obedience [Jesus] many will be made righteous. (Romans 5:19b)

If, because of one man's trespass [Adam], death reigned through that one man, much more will those who receive the abundance of grace and the free gift of righteousness reign in life through the one man Jesus Christ. (Romans 5:17)

as one man's trespass [Adam] led to condemnation for all men, so one man's act of righteousness [Jesus] leads to acquittal and life for all men. (Romans 5:18b)

"Do you see it, Ryan? Jesus' act of righteousness has led to acquittal and life for *all* men. Acquittal *and* life."

She paused to give him time as he turned his phone, opened the bible app to Romans and read the chapter. "I'm seeing the verses in a way I hadn't before," Ryan replied, realizing he needed some serious study time in Romans.

Connie smiled. "Let me take you to the punch line, Ryan. 'forget not all his benefits, who forgives all your iniquity, who heals all your diseases,'" she quoted from Psalms 103:2b-3. "This is how those benefits were given. Jesus forgives us and makes us righteous; he heals us and gives us life; and he does both for us at the cross."

Ryan looked over, startled. She'd just neatly sent him straight back to lesson one. He looked at the verses in Romans again and saw it now. *Of course.*

Connie nodded, seeing his comprehension. "At the cross Jesus forgives us and makes us righteous, to reconcile us to the father, then he heals us and he gives us life, to restore to us what is just. Jesus gives us both righteousness and what righteousness looks like. By one man's act of righteousness there is acquittal *and* life for all men.

"Jesus, at the cross, forgave every man's sins, not just ours, those who would believe in him, but the sins of the whole world. And he gave life to *all* men, because once he removed everyone's sin, he then defeated the death that came into the world through sin. Sickness and disease are simply the first visible stages that death has begun to destroy life. That's why Jesus spent his ministry years healing everyone of every disease and telling people 'your sins are forgiven, go in peace.' Jesus didn't care in which order they received his gifts, healing first, or forgiveness first. Jesus was showing what the kingdom of God looks like, what he was about to do on the cross for everyone. He was giving us the tangible reality of what it means to be forgiven of sins, to be healed, to have abundant life. Then Jesus went to the cross and he paid the price for that abundant grace to pour out upon the whole world.

"God sent his son to that cross in the hope that mankind would accept the love poured out and on display in Jesus. That's the good news of the gospel. God acted first. The most powerful words ever recorded on earth are those at the cross, "It is finished!" Jesus yanked back the earth from satan and rescued mankind. The kingdom of God restores us to who we were before sin and death entered the world. It's the brilliance of God on display.

"Jesus has forgiven and healed every person in the world. He's done it at the cross for the whole world in advance. It's a free gift of his grace. 1 Peter 2:24 says two things happened on that Friday. 'He himself bore our sins in his body on the tree' and 'By his wounds you have been healed.' Both are past tense statements. Both are inclusive of all of mankind. The Greek word for wounds is literally the stripes of scourging.

"It wasn't necessary for Jesus to get scourged in order to go to the cross, shed his blood and die to atone for our sins. So why did God the Father ask his son to go through that additional suffering? That scourging was brutal. God loves his son, He wasn't adding cruelty without a purpose. Jesus endured that scourging, he let his body be ripped apart, so our bodies could be restored from disease to health. There was a payment necessary to remove what death had done to us and Jesus paid it in full. There was no other way to restore us. That is the act of a very merciful Savior. The cross was equally cruel and also necessary, for it was the only way to make full payment for our sins. There is a powerful exchange going on. Jesus became our sin and died in our place so we could be made his righteousness. Jesus suffered in his body with the scourging so we could be healed of what death was doing to us. He made the full payment for both and then proclaimed with authority 'It is finished!' Both the complete forgiveness of our sins and complete healing of our bodies are finished works of what Jesus did for us on that Friday when he died on the cross."

She gave him a moment to think about it as she drank her coffee, then added, "Jesus doesn't make healing contingent on us, but on his work done on our behalf. Jesus spent three years healing everyone who came to him, showing us the Father's will. He's the same yesterday, today and tomorrow. He's doing the same work on our behalf now that he is on the throne. Jesus doesn't care what kind of life you've led or what you've done. If you come to Jesus, you get healed. It's a grace gift.

"The Holy Spirit who was with Jesus as he walked on the earth has been poured out upon all flesh now that Jesus is exalted in heaven and is reigning on the throne. We're healed by the same Holy Spirit as those who Jesus' touched while he was here. The Holy Spirit was poured out not because of our works or goodness or deeds. He has come as the evidence that Jesus is on the throne. The Holy Spirit dwelling in and with us is the proof text that Jesus is alive and ruling.

"Healing is a free gift we receive from Jesus' grace; we don't earn it or deserve it. He heals us because he loves us. The same with forgiveness of sins. Healing and forgiveness are free gifts available for everyone. Come to him, ask him and he heals you. He forgives you. It really is that simple. He'll heal before you believe in him, he did it all the time for people, as a proof text that he loves you. Jesus said believe me because of my words, or believe in me because of the works I do in my Father's name, just believe in me.

"It's beautiful, how God set up the gospel. The greatest news on earth is God's goodwill toward men. He forgives all our iniquity, heals all our diseases, redeems our life from the Pit, crowns us with steadfast love and mercy and satisfies us with good for as long as we live so that our youth is renewed like the eagle's – and that Friday, the cross, is how he did it. What looks like the weakest moment in history is in fact God's magnificent act of redemption and restoration of mankind. God did his part in advance, in hope that men would accept that free gift of abundant life."

Ryan had been looking to understand where Connie's confidence rested and it took less than twelve hours for God to hand him a conversation with the answer. Connie had found the cross and what God had done there in Jesus and built her confidence upon it. That truth had become the rock under her feet.

Connie smiled as she watched him thinking. "It's finished. That's the brilliance of how God did this. That fact puts to rest a lot of questions, like whether healing ended in bible days or not, because the correct answer is everything ended in bible days. Today it's just a question of do we want to receive what has already been done. Jesus smashed everything satan would ever do in all of time, freed us of every sin we would ever do in our lives, healed us of every disease we would ever face, opened the door to eternal life and did all of it on a specific Friday, on a cross, in the year A.D. 33. God isn't bound by time, he took the sins and sicknesses of all generations who would ever live and laid them on his son.

"Matthew quoting Isaiah says Jesus 'took our infirmities and bore our diseases.' (Matthew 8:17b). It's why Isaiah, looking ahead to the cross, says 'by his stripes you are healed' as a prophecy, but Peter, looking back at the cross after it has happened, says 'by his wounds you have been healed,' past tense. Isaiah saw it coming about 700 years in his future, while Peter knew it had happened in his past on that Friday in A.D. 33.

"Infirmities are the weakness and frailties that come as a result of being sick. What we think of as aging is actually mostly infirmities we live with because of accumulating disease. Jesus took both our infirmities and our diseases and got rid of them for us. He took all our sins and put them into a grave. Jesus is the one 'who forgives all your iniquities, heals all your diseases and renews your youth like the eagle's'. By his blood we are forgiven of our sins, by his body we are healed of our diseases and by his death and resurrection we have abundant eternal life. It's wonderful.

"There are two scriptures that encapsulate it which I love:

and he [Jesus] is the expiation for our sins and not for ours only but also for the sins of the whole world. (1 John 2:2)

He himself [Jesus] bore our sins in his body on the tree, that we might die to sin and live to righteousness. By his wounds you have been healed. (1 Peter 2:24)

They were coming back to the main hospital building and Connie slowed her steps. "The beauty of that is amazing. Jesus has crushed satan. Jesus now holds the keys of death. Jesus has reversed everything that sin and death brought into our lives. 'I have come that you might have life and have it abundantly.' God does all things well. And it is all a free gift from his grace, a lavish free gift. Those who choose to believe what Jesus has done have abundant life now and eternal life forever, for the just shall live by faith."

Ryan wanted to take every detail of this conversation back apart and think it through, for the conclusions astonished him. Connie was reading it right and yet he'd never realized it until today. He would have said God healed people because he loved them, cared about them, but he had not before realized the reason was connected directly to that Friday and the cross. Every healing for every person in the world had already been accomplished, it just needed to be accepted; and what a thought that was to grasp!

Connie stopped and nodded west. "That has to be it for now, I need to go."

****

"Consider this a continuation of this morning's conversation if you have time."

"I do," Ryan replied and settled in to listen.

"Jesus secured the five benefits God has for us on the Friday he died at the cross. By Jesus' shed blood we are forgiven of our sins, by his wounded body we are healed of our diseases, by his death and resurrection we have abundant life now and eternal life in God's presence forever. God designed it so the benefits flow to individuals through that cross. Paul says the word of the cross is literally the power of God to us who are being saved. Communion is how we participate in the cross and receive its benefits."

Communion. Ryan found himself both surprised and not, by where this conversation was flowing. He hadn't understood this either. He would have sighed, but it no longer surprised him that there were entire layers to his faith that he hadn't grasped, that Connie had either figured out or herself been taught. The benefits were at the cross, so communion would be the logical connecting thread.

"Some scriptures to start with that set the foundation," Connie offered.

For I received from the Lord what I also delivered to you, that the Lord Jesus on the night when he was betrayed took bread and when he had given thanks, he broke it and said, "This is my body which is for you. Do this in remembrance of me." In the same way also the cup, after supper, saying, "This cup is the new covenant in my blood. Do this, as often as you drink it, in remembrance of me." For as often as you eat this bread and drink the cup, you proclaim the Lord's death until he comes. (1 Corinthians 11:23-26)

And the Holy Spirit also bears witness to us; for after saying, "This is the covenant that I will make with them after those days, says the Lord: I will put my laws on their hearts and write them on their minds," then he adds, "I will remember their sins and their misdeeds no more." (Hebrews 10:15-17)

in Christ Jesus you are all sons of God, through faith. (Galatians 3:26b)

For as many of you as were baptized into Christ have put on Christ. (Galatians 3:27)

We were buried therefore with him [Jesus] by baptism into death, so that as Christ was raised from the dead by the glory of the Father, we too might walk in newness of life. (Romans 6:4)

May the God of peace himself sanctify you wholly; and may your spirit and soul and body be kept sound and blameless at the coming of our Lord Jesus Christ. He who

calls you is faithful and he will do it. (1 Thessalonians
5:23-24)

"There is only one place in the New Testament that
talks about why Christians get sick. The Holy Spirit told
Paul to write the Corinthian church and tell them what the
problem was, why they were getting sick, chronically sick
and dying early. It's in first Corinthians eleven. The Holy
Spirit said it was because they weren't taking communion
properly. They weren't taking it in a worthy manner and
they didn't understand the difference between the body and
the blood. Jesus' blood was for the forgiveness of sins,
while Jesus' body was broken for their healing. They
thought both his body and blood were for the forgiveness of
their sins. They weren't discerning the parts of communion
as being separate gifts. But scriptures show the body and
the blood have different functions:

the blood of Jesus his Son cleanses us from all sin. (1
John 1:7b)

By his wounds you have been healed. (1 Peter 2:24b)

"They didn't understand what Jesus had done for
them, how to receive the life he had given them. They were
acting as if communion was a ritual, nothing of present
meaning to them but a history note in their gatherings, not
realizing it was the transmission method for Christ's life to
them."

Ryan didn't wince, but he would have raised his hand
and admitted he hadn't understood that either, though it
was obvious to him now as she said it. Communion had
been a time to be sorry for what he had done, to apologize
for the sins that had made it necessary for Jesus to go to the
cross, to thank Jesus for taking his place and saving his life.
All well and good. He'd understood the blood of Jesus
cleansing him from his sins, but couldn't remember ever
thinking about Jesus' gift of his body as a unique fact

involved in his healing. If it had even been taught, the lesson hadn't registered with him. How many years of communion had it been without understanding the full picture? Thirty? Ryan pushed away the sadness of that to focus on what Connie was offering with this conversation.

"Jesus understood what communion would be to us and was talking about it in depth even before he went to the cross. Listen to some statements of Jesus:

I am the bread of life. (John 6:48)

he who eats me will live because of me. (John 6:57b)

the bread which I shall give for the life of the world is my flesh. (John 6:51b)

unless you eat the flesh of the Son of man and drink his blood, you have no life in you (John 6:53b)

He who eats my flesh and drinks my blood abides in me and I in him. (John 6:56)

"Jesus was talking about communion. With communion we proclaim Jesus' death and resurrection until he comes, but it is much deeper than that. Communion is when we come into union with Christ. As Paul expressed it in 1 Corinthians 10:16: 'The cup of blessing which we bless, is it not a participation in the blood of Christ? The bread which we break, is it not a participation in the body of Christ?' We come into the divine exchange with Jesus during communion."

Connie gave him a moment to consider those words, then held out her hand and let the sunlight brighten her skin. "Look at the light I'm enjoying. I am present day experiencing God's word 'Let there be light' spoken at creation. Likewise, when I take communion I am present day experiencing Jesus' words from A.D. 33 'he who eats me will live because of me.' Jesus was speaking the

Father's words by the Holy Spirit, for Jesus said 'I have not spoken on my own authority; the Father who sent me has himself given me commandment what to say and what to speak.' (John 12:49).

"What Jesus was describing with communion was the Father's design for how we receive what the cross does for us. The act of eating the bread is to be done with the words in mind, 'I am the bread of life', 'This is my body for you', 'By his wounds you have been healed', so that we eat with faith (trust) in those words and we receive that life offered. Likewise, when we drink the cup, it's to be with the words in mind, 'this is the new covenant in my blood'. That new covenant that says, 'I will be your God and you shall be my people. I will remember your sins and their misdeeds no more.' Communion is incredibly powerful when taken with understanding faith.

"God likes symmetry. Adam and Eve brought sin and death into the world by what they ate. God arranged his answer so that what we eat, the bread that is his son's body and what we drink, the cup that is his son's blood, would reverse what sin and death have done to us. God turned the act of eating that was disobedience, into an act of obedience which sets us free.

"Jesus' words 'he who eats me will live because of me' are carrying the power of life with them. When we participate in communion, discerning the difference between the bread and blood, receiving both gifts – forgiveness and healing – communion accomplishes what God the Father designed; it brings to us life. God's word is living and active. It always has been. And it means what it literally says, 'he who *eats* me will live because of me'. Healing is in the bread of communion. And we have mostly missed seeing it.

"By taking communion without understanding, seeing it as a ritual without practical meaning in their lives, the Corinthian Christians were setting themselves up to be sick, chronically sick and to die early. They weren't receiving what communion was designed to bring them. They were not seeing it as a living act. They were not discerning the difference in the two gifts, the body given for their healing and the blood given for their forgiveness.

"It's the same for us today. If we don't take communion discerning both the body and the blood and come to communion to receive life, we are cutting ourselves off from the ongoing life that is intended to keep us healed and healthy for the rest of our lives."

Connie paused, turning her hand to watch the sunlight highlight her spread fingers, before lowering her hand and looking over at him. "As I understand scripture, communion is the primary way God heals and keeps Christians healthy. The laying on of hands is the primary way God heals unbelievers—he uses an act of faith by a believer to help an unbeliever. The word of authority and the prayer of faith work equally well to heal both groups."

Ryan nodded at that useful summary.

Connie shifted on the bench, her voice turning even more reflective. "God, in Christ, finished his perfect plan. The five benefits of being God's people—he forgives all our sins and heals all our diseases, being the first two— came through Jesus and the cross. They flow through communion to us. The benefits are grace gifts. We don't receive any of them by our works. Not many people realize you can't, by your works, be healthy. To try is to actually guarantee you won't be. But that's a conversation for another day.

"'...the word of the cross is folly to those who are perishing, but to us who are being saved it is the power of God.' (1 Corinthians 1:18b) Jesus dealt with sin, sickness and disease for us. It's his victory. It's not our ongoing fight. The battle is finished. We need to let that light get into us. We need to know the truth, for the truth sets us free. If you're sick, a good place to start is to take communion with every meal, come into union with Christ by faith and receive from him life.

"Jesus said he came 'to seek and save the lost.' (Luke 19:10b) We need to let him. The world is lost because they haven't understood forgiveness, they think they have to work to earn it rather than receive it as a free gift. Christians are mostly lost because they haven't understood how to be healed and made whole. The answer for us is the same as for the world, come to Jesus and receive grace for all our needs.

"Saved in the Greek is so comprehensive a word it is hard to list all the meanings in English—delivered, forgiven, healed, made whole—saved is being restored fully to life. We tend to only think of forgiveness, when God has provided so much more. All our needs in life are answered in Jesus. Second Corinthians says even the money we need comes directly from what Jesus did for us that Friday. Our answers run straight through the cross. It's Paul's core message, 'by grace you have been saved through faith' (Ephesians 2:8) We need Jesus, to see with understanding him both crucified and resurrected. After that we need to open our eyes and realize Jesus is now a King. And Kings rule. But that's also a conversation for another day."

Connie went quiet for a long moment and Ryan could see the tiredness in her pressing down after a long day of work. He chose to silence his own questions. Now wasn't the time.

She glanced his way, offered a sad smile. "We have a bad habit, Ryan. When one of those benefits isn't reaching us, we come up with theories for why God's word isn't true. We don't ask him what the problem is and press through to the answer he has for us.

"It grieves God's heart to see people sick when Jesus paid the price to make everyone healthy. His heart aches to see how many will go to hell when Jesus paid to save everyone's life. God told his sons, us, to share the gospel. This generation of the church, we've mostly forgotten what that good news actually is."

Ryan didn't try to find words to describe what he was feeling. It was her most somber message so far, even as the content was some of the richest. He'd never seen the connections before. And the conviction he felt was like the Holy Spirit had taken fire from God's altar and let it fall on him. "We're that Corinthian church."

Connie nodded. "We're the generation of Christians who are sick, chronically sick and dying early."

He quietly closed the recording, thinking it through. "I need to start bringing communion to the Christians in my hospital every day."

Connie's smile lightened. "You'll get there, Ryan, but not in a day, or even a few days. The Corinthian believers were taking communion and it wasn't profiting them because they didn't understand it. You've got to know the word, get it in your own heart, train a few others, bring communion to people and in the method of sharing communion raise their understanding so they can participate with faith."

"I'm a man who can, with God's grace, figure out how to do that. Thanks for giving me the extra time today."

Connie offered a tired shrug. "Jesus said, 'let's take a walk' and I said 'okay'. We ended up here. If I'm going to sit and enjoy your garden, even while it's mostly still in winter stillness, I figure it's only fair I give you something back."

"Where to next?"

"Home."

****

Ryan Notes / conversation four / additional references

For the word of the cross is folly to those who are perishing, but to us who are being saved it is the power of God. (1 Corinthians 1:18)

And many followed him [Jesus] and he healed them all and ordered them not to make him known. This was to fulfil what was spoken by the prophet Isaiah: "Behold, my servant whom I have chosen,

my beloved with whom my soul is well pleased.
I will put my Spirit upon him,
and he shall proclaim justice to the Gentiles.
He will not wrangle or cry aloud,
nor will any one hear his voice in the streets;
he will not break a bruised reed
or quench a smoldering wick,
till he brings justice to victory;
and in his name will the Gentiles hope."
Then a blind and dumb demoniac was brought to him and
he healed him, so that the dumb man spoke and saw. And
all the people were amazed and said, "Can this be the Son
of David?" (Matthew 12:15b-23)

I [Jesus] am the bread of life. (John 6:48)

"I [Jesus] am the living bread which came down from
heaven; if any one eats of this bread, he will live for ever;
and the bread which I shall give for the life of the world is
my flesh." (John 6:51)

Truly, truly, I [Jesus] say to you, unless you eat the flesh of
the Son of man and drink his blood, you have no life in
you; (John 6:53b)

He who eats my flesh and drinks my blood abides in me
and I [Jesus] in him. (John 6:56)

As the living Father sent me and I [Jesus] live because of
the Father, so he who eats me will live because of me.
(John 6:57)

The cup of blessing which we bless, is it not a participation
in the blood of Christ? The bread which we break, is it not
a participation in the body of Christ? (1 Corinthians 10:16)

For I [Paul] received from the Lord what I also delivered to
you, that the Lord Jesus on the night when he was betrayed

took bread and when he had given thanks, he broke it and said, "This is my body which is for you. Do this in remembrance of me." In the same way also the cup, after supper, saying, "This cup is the new covenant in my blood. Do this, as often as you drink it, in remembrance of me." For as often as you eat this bread and drink the cup, you proclaim the Lord's death until he comes. Whoever, therefore, eats the bread or drinks the cup of the Lord in an unworthy manner will be guilty of profaning the body and blood of the Lord. Let a man examine himself and so eat of the bread and drink of the cup. For any one who eats and drinks without discerning the body eats and drinks judgment upon himself. That is why many of you are weak and ill and some have died. But if we judged ourselves truly, we should not be judged. But when we are judged by the Lord, we are chastened so that we may not be condemned along with the world. (1 Corinthians 11:23-32)

He himself [Jesus] bore our sins in his body on the tree, that we might die to sin and live to righteousness. By his wounds you have been healed. (1 Peter 2:24)

If the Spirit of him who raised Jesus from the dead dwells in you, he [God] who raised Christ Jesus from the dead will give life to your mortal bodies also through his Spirit which dwells in you. (Romans 8:11)

"O death, where is thy victory? O death, where is thy sting?" The sting of death is sin and the power of sin is the law. But thanks be to God, who gives us the victory through our Lord Jesus Christ. (1 Corinthians 15:55-57)

****

Ryan held out his phone, having begun the recording. "Would you talk to me more about Joy and what happened?"

"Sure, it dovetails nicely into what I thought would be today's topic." Connie gestured with her coffee. "You've seen most of it already, Ryan. Visible sickness and disease is death beginning to destroy life. Jesus is alive. He's King. He's forgiven all sin. He's now holding the keys of death. All authority in heaven and earth has been given to Jesus. Notice who has no authority anymore? Satan. Death. They no longer have a legal right to touch a person. Knowing those facts, I brought the King's reign to the situation. 'In Jesus name, death, get your hands off Joy.'

"Death leaves when you tell it to, Ryan. It's what Jesus meant when he said 'I will give you the keys of the kingdom of heaven' (Matthew 16:19) What are the keys Jesus is holding? The keys of death and hades. The right to bind on earth what has been bound in heaven, the right to loose on earth what has been loosed in heaven.

"We are announcing the judgment of the King. We're the spokesman who speaks with the delegated authority of King Jesus. We speak his will, in his name and it's done on earth as it is in heaven. We're not making up what we personally think might be interesting to have happen; we're acting with authority because we're under authority. He wants his will done on earth, as it is in heaven—and that's the whole ballgame. There's no sickness in heaven. And the earth is now under Jesus' full authority.

"'By his wounds you have been healed' is a statement of fact. Jesus is the Victor in this massive collision of kingdoms which occurred. Jesus has decided that he will act on earth through the words and actions of his disciples. He waits for us to step into our responsibility. Healing simply requires us to go deliver what Jesus has done. We're announcing the victory of the King over sickness, disease and death."

Ryan found the kingdom collision description very helpful. "Would you describe the prayer you said? I wish I had been there to get it recorded."

Connie laughed softly. "For that reason alone, I'm glad you weren't. You would try to copy my words rather than give your own. I told death to get his hands off Joy in Jesus' name. I rebuked disease in her body and told it to get out. I blessed her in Jesus' name. I asked the Holy Spirit to fill her, to give her his overflowing abundant life. I asked Jesus to comfort all who entered her room. Then I asked the Holy Spirit to teach and guide all her caregivers while Joy was their patient. I said Amen, which means 'so be it'; it's like the judge's gavel coming down. Then I said thank you to God, because I knew God had just done what I asked. And because we both enjoy it, I sang God a song of thanks as I walked home and celebrated in advance what would unfold in the hours to come.

"I exercised faith, Ryan. The words I spoke came from my heart. Came from the truth I know. I said what was going to happen and the Holy Spirit gave my words authority because I am an adopted son of God. Everything in the invisible and visible world reacted to my words and complied with the orders. Death took his hands off her. Disease left. Life flowed into her. Healing prayer isn't difficult, you simply have to know what the will of God is on the matter of healing, then go speak from his delegated authority as a son of God. Jesus healed everyone of every disease—that's the standard. We are to go and do the same.

"Sometimes it helps to close my eyes and simply put my attention on Jesus, rather than look at who I'm seeking to have healed. The invisible is the real and lasting world; this one we see is changeable. The invisible world is the truth, God's domain. This world we physically see is more like facts. It is real – you can touch, taste, see, smell and feel it – but it is changeable. Facts can be changed. God's truth, his kingdom, never changes.

"The invisible world created this visible one. The laws of the invisible world are more powerful than the laws of the natural visible world. The invisible world is the parent and the visible one the child; the child obeys the parent. Think of it this way. Gravity is a powerful law. But the law of lift can enable a plane to fly, as if gravity didn't exist for the plane. In the same way, spiritual laws don't negate natural ones, they simply come in over them and can do something which natural laws can't do.

"God heals by both natural laws, our immune system kills a germ, for example and by spiritual laws. Jesus speaks and a blind man sees – that's a spiritual law in action. God is quite comfortable healing in either way, for he created both the visible and invisible worlds, natural and spiritual. They are all his methods and laws and ways of working. It's not just natural laws which work on earth; it is who is speaking and acting that gives a law its effect.

"Think of a miracle as a healing which happens in a compressed time period. Or one which requires an act of creation to occur, a blind eye now sees. If the healing comes through a natural law which God energizes, or by a miracle, a spiritual law is applied, that is up to God. I know the truth I am speaking. In Jesus name, this person is healed. I know what healed looks like and that is where my confidence rests. What I am speaking in Jesus' name is what God has done for this person through Jesus' grace. I know what the outcome of being healed looks like.

"I was praying over Joy, but mostly I was simply taking action as the spokesperson for Jesus. I already knew what he wanted done, so I did it in his name. I spoke to death. I spoke to disease. I spoke to the Holy Spirit and to Jesus and said what I wanted to happen. I wasn't ever really asking God would you like to do this thing I'm asking? I simply directed. I'm humbly gracious when my words are directed to the Holy Spirit, to Jesus and curt with death and disease, for I know to whom I'm speaking. But I never really asked anything during that prayer, I simply said what would happen. And said Amen confident what I said I received. We're now watching it unfold and become visible. Joy will grow stronger until she's healed, barring anything intervening which squashes the prayer I said. Which itself is a topic for another day.

"I acted as Jesus would have in that situation. He would have phrased things differently, but Jesus is fine with my personality shaping how I choose to express his words and will. The gospels of Matthew, Mark, Luke and John sound like the guys who wrote them, but all are the inspired word of God. I speak from the comfortable footing of knowing who Jesus is and what he wants done in this situation. If I'm not sure, I go talk to God until I am. Asking prayer, petitioning prayer, looking for understanding, that's what you do before you enter a situation that needs you to act. Healing is an action, a proclamation, a direction. In Jesus' name, I say what is to happen."

Connie gestured toward the garden park so their walk could continue another six minutes, granting an extension she'd have to make up from her own morning schedule. Ryan gratefully nodded his thanks and turned that way with her.

"That prayer for Joy is what the Holy Spirit does. He teaches us to do what Jesus did by both explaining where the authority comes from and how we are to use it. The Holy Spirit teaches us how to get our footing. It's like the first time we stand up on a surfboard. It helps to have someone coach you through it. God did not give us a spirit of timidity but a spirit of power and love. The Holy Spirit teaches us how to get things done, how to bring the kingdom of God to earth using Jesus' name. The Holy Spirit is the one called alongside us, he's our helper, he's God who is bringing healing. He simply chooses to work with us rather than independent of us.

"Jesus never prayed for someone, he simply healed them. That was the most striking thing I noticed as I went through the gospels after George and I started talking. Jesus prayed all night on occasion. He valued prayer. But he understood that something else was needed from him when he was dealing with sickness. He said what would happen and it was done. He had authority as the son of God. He destroyed the works of the devil not by petitioning the Father to act, but by stating what the Father wanted done and the Holy Spirit gave his words power. Jesus was a man like us, speaking with the authority of a son of God, with the Holy Spirit resting upon him. That's the definition of a believer today, an adopted son of God, the Holy Spirit with us and dwelling in us.

"I'll often ask the Holy Spirit when I'm with someone, 'what else do I need to do?' I'm looking for insight into what he sees. Sometimes you tell infection to die; sometimes you tell white blood cells to multiply in numbers. It's not unusual for the Holy Spirit to give ideas that use the knowledge you have of anatomy or disease so you give very specific directions. I've heard surgeons tell specific ligaments to heal, specific blood vessels and because they are speaking in Jesus' authority, that's what happens.

"We grow more confident the more we do. It's like a child with training wheels on their bike, who will wobble at first without them, but then finds their balance. How you learn is by doing."

Connie paused and smiled. "By the way—the Holy Spirit teaches children to say healing prayers easier than he teaches adults. Children expect they can learn things they haven't yet mastered; adults have already decided they can't do it. An eight year old who knows Jesus is King can order cancer to get out in Jesus name easier than an adult. They know a King's name is all powerful and still grasp with a child's faith the understanding that the invisible rules the visible. Supernatural things happening are still within a child's comfort zone.

"You learn how to do stuff in the kingdom of God by looking to Jesus and what he did, by reading the book of Acts and watching the early church thrive using Jesus' name to act." She paused and Ryan could see her searching for how to sum up what she understood.

"It comes back to the basic fact the word is living and active. The Holy Spirit wrote the word and is your personal teacher. He explains it in ways you can understand. He knows how you are perceiving a lesson. He knows where you've grasped the truth as he intended and where your understanding is partially there and when you're simply not seeing and understanding something he wants you to know. That's okay. It's the Holy Spirit's job to teach you everything you will need to know about being a Christ follower. He'll keep coming back to a lesson until we understand what he wants us to grasp.

"When the Holy Spirit looks at us, even when we are 100 years of age, we're still going to look young to him. The Holy Spirit has volunteered to be with us for eternity and his name isn't going to change. He will still be our teacher and our guide, our comforter and our helper. The one called alongside to be our advocate, when we are a million years old. That's why Jesus says you need to be a child to enter the kingdom of God. You need to still be willing to learn, to take risks, to trust the God who is teaching you. Who is working with you to help you grow to maturity. To trust his good heart toward you. They know what they're doing. We have to let them—the Father, Jesus, the Holy Spirit—be God and if they say jump, we jump. You learn by doing. It's the definition of who we are, his people obey his voice."

Ryan was fascinated by that explanation. "Thanks, Connie."

****

"The topic for tonight's walk is faith."

Connie gave him a moment to mentally shift gears to that particular subject. He nodded, already thinking this was going to be an interesting walk.

"So let's start with a couple scriptures:

faith comes from what is heard and what is heard comes by the preaching of Christ. (Romans 10:17b)

without faith it is impossible to please him. For whoever would draw near to God must believe that he exists and that he rewards those who seek him. (Hebrews 11:6b)

"Christians often think they have to come up with faith, that it's something they have to mentally will themselves to have. 'Okay, I've convinced myself these verses I wonder about are actually true, so now I'll hurry and pray with faith.' They try to stay on that mental balancing beam long enough to pray and hopefully get their answer from God before their doubt overwhelms the faith they had worked up. They've missed a major point of truth and have also moved themselves back under the law, thinking they have to work to get faith.

"Faith is a gift given by grace; like the forgiveness of sins, it's free and it's something that is from God. Faith just comes in a unique way. You receive faith by hearing the word of God. You hear the word and it's like faith is sticking to the letters. Faith comes to you by what you hear, it's brought to you by the word of God. This living active word of God changes us by something that comes along with the word.

"Faith comes. Faith arrives. Faith shows up. Keep reading the word of God, hearing it, thinking about it, quoting it back to yourself so you can hear it with your ears as well as read it with your eyes. There will be a moment where you'll suddenly realize 'I get it, I understand this, I trust this,' and you'll realize faith has shown up. Our mind is renewed with the truth of the word, while faith accumulates in our heart as we understand the word. Both the word of God and faith are alive, they are powerful things which change us by their presence. Faith is quiet in its arrival, but powerful in what it will then want to do. You'll move mountains after faith has arrived and will do so without doubts. Scripture is full of that intersection of having faith—trusting God—and that faith propelling you to go out and do stuff.

For time would fail me to tell of Gideon, Barak, Samson, Jephthah, of David and Samuel and the prophets – who through faith conquered kingdoms, enforced justice, received promises, stopped the mouths of lions, quenched raging fire, escaped the edge of the sword, won strength out of weakness, became mighty in war, put foreign armies to flight. (Hebrews 11:32b-34)

"Because of their faith, they went out and did things. The start of the next verse – 'Women received their dead by resurrection' – how cool is that? Faith is powerful. Faith also allows us to stand firm with God. Even when the situations unfolding around us seem like crushing defeats, faith gives us God's perspective. It's critical to our success that we understand what faith is, how it comes, what it does and how it does what it does. Christians are to both know God and be active because they know God. Christians are to be doers of the word. You can't just mentally believe and think that's a living faith. Faith is either active doing works or it has died. And a dead faith isn't going to get you into heaven. Mental knowledge alone is death to us. To know, but not be doing, means we are only deceiving ourselves.

"Faith is completed by works. Faith gets traction in us and finishes transforming us only when it is active. Muscles that atrophy can't lift anything. Muscles which are worked daily can move weight with ease. Faith is similar. Faith which is alive is doing things and growing stronger with use. We are to 'be' Christians—it's identity, character—but it's also 'be doers', it's who we are in motion, it's what we're doing in our lives. As James says, we are blessed 'in our doing'. We will be people showing our faith by our actions.

"Follow it in the scriptures:

receive with meekness the implanted word, which is able to save your souls. But be doers of the word and not hearers only, deceiving yourselves. For if any one is a hearer of the word and not a doer, he is like a man who observes his natural face in a mirror; for he observes himself and goes away and at once forgets what he was like. But he who looks into the perfect law, the law of liberty and perseveres, being no hearer that forgets but a doer that acts, he shall be blessed in his doing. (James 1:21b-25)

Do you want to be shown, you shallow man, that faith apart from works is barren? Was not Abraham our father justified by works, when he offered his son Isaac upon the altar? You see that faith was active along with his works and faith was completed by works and the scripture was fulfilled which says, "Abraham believed God and it was reckoned to him as righteousness"; and he was called the friend of God. You see that a man is justified by works and not by faith alone. And in the same way was not also Rahab the harlot justified by works when she received the messengers and sent them out another way? For as the body apart from the spirit is dead, so faith apart from works is dead. (James 2:20-26)

By faith Sarah herself received power to conceive, even when she was past the age, since she considered him faithful who had promised. (Hebrews 11:11)

As the outcome of your faith you obtain the salvation of your souls. (1 Peter 1:9)

"A living active faith wants to do something. It sees needs and opportunities and internally nudges you to act; 'let's pray for that person to be healed, invite that person to church, sign up for the youth leader training, answer that opportunity to give to the missionaries in Chile.' Not every opportunity that crosses your path is something you raise your hand to and say yes. There are ones that Jesus has in mind for you, those that hit a passion that just resonates inside you. You say yes and your faith gets excited and dives in and your actions blossom into good works. That's a living faith. You find life challenging, stretching, fun, you're growing like mad and relying on God and lives are getting changed – you're tasting living in the kingdom of God and it feels really good to you. You want more of this. You're coming alive as a Christian because your faith is flourishing."

"Anyway…the opposite of a living faith is dead faith. Faith that is dead has no works. People don't plan to end up in the situation with dead faith in their heart, but it happens frequently. Jesus was constantly on his 12 guys for having no faith, for letting their faith die, you of little faith. Tending to faith is our responsibility. It's critically important that we watch to make sure our faith doesn't die. Faith dies because it gets suppressed, poisoned, or crushed. Those problems deserve some detail, but I'm not going to go that direction tonight. I'll sum up this first part with a verse:

We are bound to give thanks to God always for you, brethren, as is fitting, because your faith is growing abundantly and the love of every one of you for one another is increasing. (2 Thessalonians 1:3)

"That's what you want to see when you look in the mirror. Faith comes as a grace gift as we read the word. Faith lives in our heart and it's our job to tend it, to let that faith do stuff. Where people misunderstand Christianity is they think being a Christian is a lot of their own effort, that it is a lot of constant hard work. In fact, God is doing the work. That new life inside you is powerful. Faith comes when you read the word and that faith is alive: it is constantly nudging you, 'let's go do this', 'let's go do that' – the impulse isn't coming from you, it's coming from faith. There's an eager joy in it, an anticipation, 'that looks challenging and fun, let's go dive in and do it'. If you cooperate with what is welling up inside you, your faith gets you involved in stuff and you blossom as you tackle things that require God to show up.

"Nothing is more thrilling than doing something and realizing God is with you in the doing. It has become a supernatural thing. If you don't suppress what God is doing, you will grow and flourish very quickly. Your faith rockets up into sturdy mature trees. You'll easily say yes to harder and harder challenges because your growing faith is more than a match for what is needed.

"It's uncomfortable trying to hold back faith from acting. There's a constant tension inside as your spirit and soul wrestle for control of who you will be. One side or the other always wins. You become like Christ, or you kill this new life inside you and turn back to the world. God doesn't let you hug the middle. Over the course of a lifetime, the only ones who endure to the end are those who have elected to become like Christ."

They were within sight of the concert venue and the sidewalk around them was flowing with people heading that direction. She nodded to the recording, signaling she was done for now.

"Thanks, Connie." Ryan closed the recording.

"I like this topic. The next conversation is back to being practical; this was more theory. I previously assumed people understood faith, but it's an area where there is often more misunderstanding than clarity. It's hard to talk about praying with faith if you haven't realized faith itself is a grace gift from God."

"I'll look forward to that conversation, too. They've all been helpful, if in different ways."

"I haven't forgotten where you want to go, Ryan," Connie mentioned, "to the big questions of opening the eyes of the blind, the lame walking, raising the dead, doing supernatural stuff, but for that conversation to be useful to you, I have to show you how to get there."

"How close are we?"

"A week."

He was startled enough he stopped walking, causing people behind him to have to rapidly react to avoid bumping into him.

Connie turned back toward him and smiled. "I didn't say you would have understood it to the point you have faith to do supernatural things, but yeah, about a week."

He felt like he'd just done a belly flop. Without implicitly saying so, she was saying she had raised the dead, opened the eyes of the blind, done the supernatural in Jesus' name. "Okay. That just motivated your student quite a bit."

She laughed. "Come on," she waved him to start walking again. "Concert venue, good music. Learn to love worship, Ryan and people who don't know Jesus yet. This is where Jesus hangs out on a Friday night. This is his kind of crowd."

Ryan fell back in step beside her, hoping he was ready for where she was taking him, both this evening and in the coming week.

11

"Would you like me to pray for your ears to stop ringing?"

Ryan laughed at Connie's kindly worded question. He gladly pitched the earplugs he had worn into the trash can at the entrance. A full moon was out. "You were absolutely enjoying every minute of that concert."

"I like loud music."

"The percussion was enough to make even Ben vibrate." The six-year-old son of the band member playing the keyboards had progressively lost his hearing since age four, was now profoundly deaf, but he'd been having a great time without needing to hear the music, able to dance around in the open area between the front row and the stage, using the crowd as his own visible music to enjoy.

Connie smiled. "That's a boy who will have no trouble falling asleep in the car on the way home."

"You've been praying for Ben's hearing to return."

"Of course." Connie retrieved the last cookie in her provisions and broke it in half to share. "I will pray for you until you are healed and if you die before that happens, I will pray to raise you from the dead." She said it with a smile, but she wasn't joking. "Ryan, a simple rule of thumb: if it's good, it's God, if it's bad, it's the other guy. The thief comes to steal, kill and destroy. Jesus comes to give abundant life.

"Satan stole Ben's healing. It's like a slap in the face to the band. He couldn't knock one of them out, so he went after a family member. Ben will get his hearing back because that's God's will in the matter and one of God's benefits to him. In the process, I'll learn how to do something I didn't know how to do before.

"By watching Jesus, I've learned never to look at a problem and think that's just the way life happens, or that a problem is permanent. Nothing in the visible world is permanent, it all gives way to the invisible world's verdict.

"His parents are probably the key that opens the lock, as parents have a very unique authority over what occurs with their children. Music is part of it, too, I think. To bring Ben to the concerts is one of the recent impressions both his mom and I got when praying for him. I know the atmosphere of praise is powerful and when the gospel is preached by music, by testimony, the Holy Spirit is very active in the crowd. Ben can't hear the music, but he enjoys the concerts. And if what I suspect has happened, Ben's got an afflicting spirit affecting his hearing; spending Friday nights at a nearly three-hour-long loud concert glorifying Jesus, has been the most miserable hours of that demon's existence to date.

"The woman in the synagogue who was stooped and bent over, couldn't straighten, Jesus set her free of the affliction and said satan had bound her for eighteen years. Jesus said 'enough!' and ended the woman's suffering and she was able to stand up straight again. She had an afflicting spirit binding her. Something similar is probably happening in Ben's case."

Connie gave him a thoughtful look. "I can see the discomfort; I'm treading into topics you don't normally consider."

Ryan could think of several ways to answer that but chose to simply shrug. "I'll adjust."

She smiled. "Most of what you deal with in healing the sick is going to be disease, something death brought in, that needs removed. But occasionally that approach yields no answer. Don't give up; instead, step back and consider what else might be going on. It's worth solving that puzzle when it presents itself. Think of Ben's situation as an advance level course, a topic I wouldn't have normally introduced you to this early. Jesus removed unclean sprits as well as healed the sick and often the presenting symptoms looked similar. The Holy Spirit helps us figure out what we're dealing with. The final outcome is the same, the person is healed." Connie shifted the backpack and pulled out another water bottle. "You were a good sport to come tonight."

"If I missed these opportunities, I'd miss getting glimpses into that range of topics you are sorting out when to discuss. And I'd miss meeting the Bens in your life."

"Let me give you one key that you might have enough to recognize now. Ryan, when you think of Ben, do you think of him as deaf?"

"He is deaf."

"That's a fact, but its not who he is. I see Ben, a normal hearing child, who has a problem blocking his hearing."

Ryan felt her words register as a solid punch. "I think of him as deaf. You think of him as hearing."

Connie nodded. "When you tie the label of the disease and the person together, you can, without realizing it, subconsciously agree with the fact the situation is permanent. It makes it incredibly hard to pray with faith once you've internalized that what you are dealing with is a permanent condition.

"A key to healing is to see the person in front of you as God does, healthy, normal, thriving with life, who temporarily has – name the condition – which needs to be removed."

"That gem right there was worth the concert."

"We can just walk if you like. There's a point where you've earned the right to say that's enough for now."

"I like listening to you Connie. You're like this entirely different universe compared to where I normally circle."

She laughed at that image. "Okay, then let's finish the topic of faith tonight and I'll try to make it worth your while."

Ryan obligingly tugged out his phone and started a recording.

"Let's start with two scriptures:

And Jesus answered them, "Have faith in God. Truly, I say to you, whoever says to this mountain, `Be taken up and cast into the sea,' and does not doubt in his heart, but believes that what he says will come to pass, it will be done for him. Therefore I tell you, whatever you ask in prayer, believe that you have received it and it will be yours. (Mark 11:24)

In the morning, as he was returning to the city, he was hungry. And seeing a fig tree by the wayside he went to it and found nothing on it but leaves only. And he said to it, "May no fruit ever come from you again!" And the fig tree withered at once. When the disciples saw it they marveled, saying, "How did the fig tree wither at once?" And Jesus answered them, "Truly, I say to you, if you have faith and never doubt, you will not only do what has been done to the fig tree, but even if you say to this mountain, `Be taken up and cast into the sea,' it will be done. And whatever you ask in prayer, you will receive, if you have faith." (Matthew 21:18-22)

"What is faith? It's the ability to 'believe that you have received it' (what you've asked) before it is in your possession. It's confidence that what you ask God is what will be done.

"Jesus asked a blind man, 'What do you want me to do for you?' He said, 'Lord, let me receive my sight.' And Jesus said to him, 'Receive your sight; your faith has made you well.' And immediately he receives his sight.

"A woman who had a flow of blood for twelve years says, 'If I touch even his garments, I shall be made well.' She comes up behind Jesus, touches the fringe of his garment and immediately her flow of blood ceases. Jesus turns and tells her, 'Daughter, your faith has made you well; go in peace.'

"Notice it was the blind man's own faith, the woman's own faith, that made them well. Jesus didn't need to add his own faith to get these healing miracles done. Their own faith was powerfully sufficient.

"The blind man came to God, said what he wanted with faith (confidence, trust) that he would receive what he said and he promptly received it. The woman healed of bleeding, acted with faith (confidence, trust) that she would receive what she had said and she promptly received it. These are teaching pictures for how our own faith operates. We ask Jesus for what we want, Jesus answers us 'receive it' at the time we ask, for he is the 'yes' to every promise of God and what we ask then shows up in our visible lives. You have faith (trust, confidence) that you will receive what you ask, that what you say is what is going to happen. You ask God for something and it shows up because you believe it will."

Ryan had heard the prayer of faith discussed many times, but her explanation was among the most precise. He nodded his thanks to Connie for that description.

She turned the topic a bit further. "God is the only being in the whole universe who can say 'ask me for anything and I'll give it' and not be lying."

Ryan smiled as Connie headed straight back to lesson one. She was delivering on her promise to offer something interesting tonight.

"God knows the end from the beginning. God has considered every possible request you will make over your entire lifetime, the entire tree of possibilities and has decided yes, I'm willing to give her everything she might ask. So God writes in his word to you, 'whatsoever you desire, when you pray, believe that you have received it and it will be yours.' (paraphrasing Mark 11:24 KJV). God has seen and pre-approved what we want to bring to him.

"Jesus reaffirms the 'anything you ask' breadth of God's offer by adding his own intent to do the same when he sits on his throne in glory, 'whatever you ask in my name, I will do it.', 'if you ask anything in my name, I will do it.' (John 14:13a,14) And just to be sure we get his point, God writes to remind us 'with God nothing will be impossible.' (Luke 1:37b) and adds for our sake, 'and nothing will be impossible to you.' (Matthew 17:20b). A son of God speaking a word with faith is given what he asks, what he says is what he receives. That is God's gift to us as his sons.

"There is really only one natural limit to what you can ask. It has to be something which exists in God's kingdom. You can't ask for a guy to be your husband when he's currently married to someone else, you can't ask for his present wife to die early—those would be examples of the other kingdom.

"Faith is not wishful thinking. 'I wish God would do this thing for me.' Faith is realizing what God has already done for you, what is sitting in the kingdom of God with your name on it and asking to receive it, to have it move from the invisible world to the visible world. The promises of God are descriptions of what is already done for you. You're forgiven, healed, delivered, blessed. Simply ask God with faith for what you desire from him and it moves from heaven to earth. God doesn't make this process of receiving difficult. God likes blessing people. The more childlike you are in heart, the easier you simply go run up to your papa and ask for what you want."

"So how do we get that faith (confidence, trust) for whatever we might ask? We've talked about how faith comes from the word of God. Faith arrives, shows up, comes to us, by what we read and understand. The specific faith for 'whatever we might ask' comes in part from these verses on prayer, from the promises we read in scripture which relate to the specifics of what we need—resources, health, direction, peace—but it also comes from understanding a comment the Holy Spirit makes about God.

his [God's] works were finished from the foundation of the world. (Hebrews 4:3b)

"This is an incredible statement about God and very useful to us when it comes to prayer.

"Let's take a simple example. You ask me for something. If I tell you I will do it and you trust me, you wait for me to act, so you can have it. Time passes. You start to wonder if I forgot, or if there was a problem, or if I just haven't gotten around to acting yet. Your anxiety rises, not because you don't trust me, but because it's important to you and it hasn't happened yet. You start debating, should I ask again? I don't want to imply she isn't trustworthy and I don't want to find out she did forget and be disappointed in her because she wasn't as faithful as I thought she was. Mentally, it turns into a mess. That situation happens all the time between people. And because that's how we've learned to think about people, we find ourselves, without intending to do so, thinking that same way about God. We asked for something, it doesn't show up immediately and we spend our lives anxious about what he did with our request.

"Scenario two – you ask me for something. If I tell you I have done it and you trust me, you simply wait for it to show up. You have 100 percent certainty it's done. You are confident it is on its way. You know I ship things by armored guards, so it's not getting lost in its delivery.

"By understanding God's works are finished from the foundation of the world, you can live in scenario two and have 100 percent certainty that what you've asked him has been done for you. Before it shows up, you are already writing the thank you note to God and preparing for what you'll do when your answer is in hand, because you know he's done what you asked. We have confident trusting faith in something that is already done, even though it hasn't shown up yet, because we believe the one who says I've done it and we know it is on its way. Listen to the verse again:

his [God's] works were finished from the foundation of the world. (Hebrews 4:3b)

"God gives us this special gift in his word, this assurance, so our lives could be peaceful in every circumstance. Life is not unfolding in a haphazard way, with God running back and forth between people and events trying to get things to work out. God is now at rest, having completed all his work. He has finished everything we need, answered every prayer, even the arrival date and time of what we have asked for has been taken care of and finished; it has all been done since the foundation of the world."

"We pray, hoping God will come through for us. God is like, 'I finished that one. Yep, that one is finished. Yep, that one, too.' If we don't pray, those answers will not come into our life. If we pray, they are guaranteed to come into our lives. How are they guaranteed? God has already done them.

"God does not lie. God does not write 'whatever you ask' without already knowing every request you will make. God has figured out how to do – and he's done – all that you will ever ask him.

"So just ask him for stuff, accept he's given it to you and relax. You'll have what you have said. It's done. Jesus lived like that. It's fascinating to watch his comfort with the world around him. Multiply bread to feed thousands? It's hand me the meal, say a simple blessing and 'okay guys, hand it out.' Lazarus has been dead four days? It's 'Lazarus, come out!' and not said in kind of a whisper so people wouldn't notice if he says it and nothing happens. It's a loud voice so all those present hear him tell the dead to wake up. That is confidence in God in action. Jesus trusted his Father. So should we. That's Jesus' message to us once we're adopted sons of God.

"'Whatever we ask' is huge, because we have a huge God. We miss something if we lower the size of his offer to something that seems reasonable to us. God is an intricate, detailed, lovely and powerful God handling the universe and all creation. God wants to fulfill what seems to us to be impossible requests to show us himself, his own nature and capacity. He doesn't need to come down to our capacity, he needs us to come up to his. Trusting him and asking him for things which allow him to be himself in your life is honoring God and who he is, it's letting him do God size things for you."

"God can tell David, a thousand years before Jesus comes to the earth, write down that they will gamble to decide who gets my son's clothing. A thousand years later Jesus dies on the cross and the soldier's are throwing dice to see who will take home Jesus' tunic. Which came first, God seeing the soldiers would throw dice, or the soldiers throwing dice and God taking note of it? Our lives are expressions of our free will, but God knows what our free will is going to choose to do. Knowing isn't causing. The two can co-exist without violating our free will, or God's omniscience.

"God can say what will happen twenty-six years from now and quote everything you will say that day, because he already knows what happens. He isn't making it happen in the sense he's controlling your free will, he's simply been in the future already and experienced that day. To him that future is present knowledge.

"We are living life thinking it is unfolding new. God is living life with us having seen all of it already. He incorporated everything we would ask him, everything we would do, everything he would do and shaped the plot to end up with the joyful marriage of his son Jesus to the radiant bride the church, with evil defeated and cast into the lake of fire.

"God relishes people who grasp his delight with them and how willing he is to answer prayers. Ask, knowing God has already finished his work to give you what you ask and you will receive what you ask. That confidence is faith. What we ask has been done. We are now just walking into the experience of it.

"The future is new to us. But it's a finished work to God. When God says 'whatever you ask in prayer, believe that you have received it and it will be yours.' (Mark 11:24b) God is telling you what he has already done in the future – it's what we've asked him for with faith."

She paused to give him a moment to think about it, then turned the subject slightly again. "We're skeptics, 'whatever you ask, that can't be true'. So we don't believe God because that statement seems impossible to us. God is trying to jar us out of that doubt in who He is so we can see the fact that it is true. God doesn't lie. Jesus' question, 'when I return, will I find faith on earth?' is poignant for a reason. Even most Christians don't believe God is telling them the truth with these verses. We live in hope we have that good of a God, while inside doubting that we do, when

God would have us live in confident certainty, knowing we do have a God who is that good. God lets you have the life you pray for, that's the hidden gift in this conversation about faith.

"It's very much like the prayer of authority, when you understand you have authority in your words as a son of God, you speak and things happen. When you ask for something in prayer with faith, something similar is happening. Faith is connecting you with God's answer. Faith is triggering, it is putting into motion, it is causing what you asked to come about. You've met the one condition God places on having whatever you ask – you've asked him with faith."

"If there is a delay, ask God what is going on; he knows. Don't simply decide your prayer was a failure. You can kill the arrival of your own answer by closing down your faith and saying 'I guess it's not going to happen'. Guess what – God will honor your words – 'it's not going to happen'. If that's your decision, that's what the result is. Sometimes the delay is God shaping you to be able to handle receiving what you've asked. Sometimes God is moving around people, your boss, your spouse, or arranging a series of events. The variety of how God delivers your answer to you is as unique as our prayers themselves are.

"God expects us to live okay with mystery, confident in Him, even when we don't see what is occurring. An enduring steady faith is what God is forming in our lives, because nothing is impossible to those who have been trained to ask and walk and live by faith."

Connie paused walking to sum up the topic. "You have authority by position, (you are a son of God) and you have ability to do by faith, (your trust in God). You speak with authority (I am a son of God speaking under delegated authority) and with faith (I trust God that what I'm about to say is what is going to happen) and you get results.

"Jesus spoke with faith when he said 'Peace! Be Still!' and his words carried with them the power to accomplish what he spoke. We're to live like that, knowing our words always yield what we say. God intends our lives to be ones of vibrant prayer, asking him for what we need and Him answering our requests. We are royal priests under Jesus and we function in that role by faith-filled prayers and actions inspired by that faith."

****

Ryan Notes / conversation five / additional references

His divine power has granted to us all things that pertain to life and godliness, through the knowledge of him who called us to his own glory and excellence, by which he has granted to us his precious and very great promises, that through these you may escape from the corruption that is in the world because of passion and become partakers of the divine nature. (2 Peter 1:3-4)

the righteousness based on faith says...the word is near you, on your lips and in your heart...; because, if you confess with your lips that Jesus is Lord and believe in your heart that God raised him from the dead, you will be saved. For man believes with his heart and so is justified and he confesses with his lips and so is saved. (Romans 10:6b-10)

For whatever is born of God overcomes the world; and this is the victory that overcomes the world, our faith. (1 John 5:4)

You do not have, because you do not ask. You ask and do not receive, because you ask wrongly, to spend it on your passions. (James 4:2b-3)

12

Saturday morning brought showers and the surprising realization he didn't have Connie's phone number. Calling the number for Connie's Pizza only got him a cheerful recording which detailed the location and hours she was open.

Ryan drove over to the coffee shop and hoped for the best regarding limited parking. He saw Connie walking toward the coffee shop carrying an umbrella, in no particular hurry compared to other pedestrians, looking actually quite comfortable decked out in warm waterproof boots and a long water slick jacket with hood, black gloves. He flashed his light and caught her attention, then lowered the passenger side window. "I'll give you a lift to Connie's Pizza in exchange for a cup of coffee there," he offered, ignoring the impatient driver behind him. Connie collapsed the umbrella and joined him in the car and Ryan chose to also ignore the gesture the driver behind him made for the thirty second pause.

"Thanks." She clipped on her seatbelt and lowered the hood, ran fingers through her hair, didn't seem bothered by the rain that had gotten past the umbrella. He circled the block to get back to Voss street and turned toward Connie's Pizza.

"I realized I didn't have your number."

"How's your memory?"

"For numbers, pretty solid."

She gave him her number. "I would have called the hospital and relayed a message if I was canceling on you."

He nodded. "I appreciate that."

"Before I forget," Connie tugged a flash drive from her pocket, "I did your homework for you. A long audio titled Saturday and also some shorter ones."

"Thanks. I'm stunned you had time to do this." He slid the flash drive into his shirt pocket for safe keeping.

"I couldn't have predicted when the ten and twenty minute gaps would show up, but there have been a few I captured for you."

He glanced over, relieved she looked less drawn than she had a couple days before. He knew her last night had been on the brief side. "Do you mind if I ask a personal question?"

"You can ask anything you like. I'm good at saying no comment. Just because you ask, doesn't mean I'll answer."

"I can live with that." There wasn't a particularly good way to ask this, so he just said the words. "How'd you sleep last night? Are you seeing a few hours of decent sleep a night, or is it still choppy? Combat medic to civilian— that's got baggage coming home with you."

She looked surprised by the question, then quietly touched, as her smile softened. "My mind is reasonably tranquil, Ryan, but thank you for asking. I'm about where most combat medics would be ten years after they leave the service. Jesus and I have a routine with memories of events that lets him sort them out for me. It's rare to need to deal with a particular memory more than a few times. And I have had George around, if not monthly, on a regular enough basis I could always get a few hours of his time. He is the best I've ever seen for helping soldiers process the mental toll being in the military creates. He now trains most of the chaplain corp on the process he uses.

"Being at peace doesn't require peaceful surroundings. Once you learn that truth, the war zone with bullets flying, the bumper-to-bumper traffic with snarled impatient drivers"—she nodded out the window—"or the quiet evening at home, can all be accommodated. I choose not to be afraid and that dramatically reduces the stress. I choose to relax and that drastically improves my ability to come up with creative decisions in any situation. I have to be busier, both mentally and physically, in a combat zone than when I'm at home lying on my couch, but I can be at peace in either place. My life is under my control even if you're trying to cause me problems. I don't have to accept what

you're doing. I've got God with me and I can deal with this
world however it needs to be dealt with. I literally have the
peace of Jesus; he's given it to me.

"Besides, I'm immortal, Ryan, eternal. What do I care
if I die today? I feel sorry for whoever has to do the
paperwork, but there are no dangling threads in my life that
are unfinished. I've told Jesus how many years I want to
live. If I die before that date, he's going to prompt someone
to pray to raise me from the dead. They may ignore the
prompting, but Jesus is good at answering my prayers by
whatever means are necessary. He'll figure something out."

They were at Connie's Pizza, so Ryan parked and let
Connie open up the shop, get lights on, turn on the oven
and start the coffee, before he asked the first of the
questions burning to be asked. While she did those items,
he set down the chairs off the tables for her. He chose a
table near the drink counter when he was done and took a
seat. "You can choose when you want to die?"

"Sure. This is like lesson ten material so you'll just
have to let me say what I say and wait for me to explain
some of it." She settled comfortably in a chair opposite him
and slipped off her boots. "I can give you until 8:40 thanks
to the enjoyable drive, but there's other stuff more
important I think you should hear today."

"I can accept that."

"God gives man free will. There are very few things
God doesn't let man decide. You can't decide when Jesus
comes back, the Father has reserved that decision to
himself. You can't decide that I will believe in Jesus, that's
my call, not yours. Everything else? Pretty much up to us.

"Joshua decided the sun wasn't going to go down. So
it didn't go down. Elijah decided it wasn't going to rain on
the earth for three and a half years. So it didn't rain. David
decided God should have a house to live in. God was
content with his tent. God said I chose the man and the man
wants to build me a house, so I'll go along with that plan.
God threw himself into the endeavor with great passion and
made the dedication of the temple David's son Solomon

built the high point of Israel's history. There's never been a point of more splendor or glory in the Old Testament. God loved that house because to build it for Him was in David's heart. That's worship expressed in a tangible way and God loved it.

"By the way—have you ever read the first tabernacle blueprints, the tent God called home before the temple was built? God loves details. 'Hey Moses, here's the blueprint for what I want my tent to look like, down to the color of the thread in the curtains.'" She laughed at the image her own words created. "And as you read, you realize every one of those details was telling us something about Jesus and the unfolding plan bringing us salvation. God loves symbolic pictures of truth.

"Anyway. From those three examples which God recorded in scripture to show us where the boundaries are of our free will, I'd say that God is letting man have enormous say in what unfolds."

Connie rose to get their coffee and brought two full mugs over to the table. "The length of our life is not set in stone in God's book. God says you're appointed once to die, but he doesn't say when. God knowing the date of your death is different from him setting it. All your decisions are factored into the date he knows.

"Hezeki'ah said I don't want to die. God said because you prayed, I'll add 15 years to your life.

"People tend to forget God's first command with promise — if you want it to go well with you and you want to live a long life on the earth, honor your parents.

"You can ask to live 120 years on the earth and God will let you. Adam lived like 900 years. The reason we can't live more than 120 years now is that God changed the limit after the Noah flood, said I'm done with men living 600, 800 years, thinking nothing but evil thoughts. I'm setting a new limit on mankind at 120 years.

"Moses, who spoke to God face-to-face, who was as righteous as a man could become under that first covenant. Guess how long he lived? 120 years.

"Scripture says Moses' eyesight was not dim, he was in good health, he climbed a mountain the day he died. God told him 'you're going to die today, so go climb that mountain, look at the promised land and then I'll take your breath away and you'll sleep with your fathers.' Moses dies at 120. Don't bother to ask for 121 years, because God's already said no. But 120 is fine.

"Paul was wrestling with when to die, torn between the beauty of heaven or the usefulness of his ministry on earth. He decided to stay longer on earth in order to keep ministering to people.

"It's like dying without a will and so the state decides what happens to your stuff, or you make a will and decide for yourself what will happen to your stuff. If you don't tell God when you want to die, then other people may choose the date. Satan may try to step in with a date. Or your own actions will accumulate and cause your body to stop functioning on some unpredictable date. When you tell God when you want to die, he'll answer your prayer and adjust your death date to match your prayer request. That doesn't mean you are a passive spectator to the process. If he says don't take that plane flight, you have to adjust your plans and not get on the plane. Life is still walked out together on how to get to that date you've asked Him to set. You cooperate with God so He can give you your request. But that's how God answers every prayer. We pray and we cooperate. God will let you decide when you die."

She leaned back in her chair, relaxed. "I'm surprised more people don't make this decision for themselves. They fret and worry about what might go wrong, 'maybe I'll have an accident and I'll die this year,' when they could have just set a date with God for the year they turn 97 and know they don't have to worry about the question. Death won't come until then, unless they tell God, 'I've changed my mind, I want to die when I'm 85, I'm tired of earth, all my friends have passed away and I want to go to heaven sooner.'"

"Connie, who taught you this? To choose the age you want to die?"

"George. He was talking to one of those 23-year-olds in the army, a young man who has just realized how close he came to getting shot and killed while on patrol that day. The young man was terrified of going back out on patrol come morning. He's certain he's going to die, he's never going to get married, have kids, have the life he's dreamed about; why was he so stupid as to think the army would be an adventure?

"George, in his calm chaplain way, listens to him for a while, then gives him a piece of advice. 'Relax, son. If you die, I'll pray to resurrect you from the dead.'

"The advice spread like a wildfire. Word gets around the unit. You need a DNR to stay dead. Otherwise, George was going to yank you from death back to life. A DNR in our parlance is Do Not Resurrect. And the corollary spreads just as fast: If you're a Christian and not too worried about dying because death gets you to heaven, you'd better file a DNR with George so you can stay there once you arrive.

"The change was like night and day. They turned into one of the most fearless units in the army. No one was afraid to die anymore. And no one did. They all headed home together eighteen months later when their tour finished."

"How many did George pray for?"

Connie smiled, but simply got up to get the coffee pot and refill their mugs. "You'll need to ask George that question. Somewhere in that stretch of time, George explained choosing the age you want to die and it had the same effect in a more permanent way. Rather than rely on a person to be there to keep his word—George being there to pray—you could just agree with God on the date and let God sort out details to get you to that age. If someone needs to pray to raise you from the dead, God will arrange for that person to be there when you need him."

"You really are comfortable with the idea of raising the dead being more than just for bible times, or a one person every hundred years rare event in Christianity."

"Answer me this, Ryan. Who holds the keys of death?"

He thought for a moment. "Jesus."

Connie nodded. "Revelation 1:18b. 'I have the keys of Death and Hades.' Who said 'whatever you ask in my name, I will do it,' said it twice in the space of 2 verses?"

"Jesus."

"Does Jesus lie?"

He smiled as she walked him straight into her first lesson. "No. Jesus does not lie."

"Jesus always did the will of the Father. And Jesus raised the dead. Scripture names 4 of those individuals and there were probably more given Jesus' comment to John's disciples. So people can die early, before it's the Father's will. Jesus was setting things right by raising them from the dead. He didn't stress over it. 'Little girl, get up.' 'Young man, I say to you rise.' 'Lazarus, come out.' It wasn't hard.

"Peter raised the dead. He prayed, then turned to Tabitha and said, 'Tabitha, rise.' She opened her eyes and when she saw him, she sat up.

"You know who else believed in raising the dead? Abraham. He took Isaac to the mountain top to kill him because God said to sacrifice his son. But Abraham told his servants we will be back, plural. He believed he would kill Isaac and God would raise him from the dead so that they would both return together. His descendents would be born through Isaac; Abraham had God's word on that. So if a resurrection is what it took for God to keep his word, then a resurrection would certainly happen. Abraham had a fearless confidence in God. He was a man who had taken into his heart the truth that God does not lie. He *never* will.

"Eli'jah and Eli'sha both raised the dead. One of the most fascinating resurrections ever recorded involves Eli'sha. He's lived his life and died, been buried for some months. There's another funeral happening in that cemetery in the spring. A marauding band of enemies is seen and the people attending scatter. The guys officiating at the funeral look around for where to put the dead man. Eli'sha's tomb is the nearest. They cast the dead man into the grave of Eli'sha and as soon as the man touches the bones of Eli'sha, he revives and stands on his feet." Connie laughed. "Now that's a quandary. What do you say to the dead guy who is now alive? 'Run! They're going to kill anyone they catch.' If he doesn't run fast, the man is going to die twice in the same twenty-four hours. That's just really bad timing." She chuckled. "Anyway...

"God himself obviously believes in raising the dead. God the Father was foreshadowing with Abraham and Isaac what He himself would do with Jesus. The Father would one day sacrifice his own beloved son then resurrect him and use that act as the means to save the entire world.

"People haven't stopped dying early, Ryan, before it's the will of the Father. Just look at the children dead of gunshot violence in Chicago. None of those deaths are the Father's will. The thief came to steal, kill and destroy and we let him.

"The real question is—why aren't we doing the will of the Father like Jesus did? Jesus came to destroy the works of the devil. Jesus hasn't changed. He uses us now; we are his co-laborers. We are the body of Christ here on earth. We aren't passive spectators. It's our job to bring about the Father's will on earth using Jesus' name. When we see someone who died early, we should set things right by raising them from the dead."

"It is fascinating to listen to you. You really are comfortable with this subject."

"Had we arrived at it in the correct order of lessons you wouldn't be surprised at what you heard today, nor why I'm comfortable with the subject." She tipped her mug toward him. "You missed it, didn't you? I don't mean that question in an 'I'm disappointed in you' kind of way, but I'm always puzzled why it happens. In all the conversation going by you on the topic you've been most interested in, you still missed the answer you've been eagerly wanting to learn."

Ryan went still. "Keep talking, please."

"Ryan, who wants to do God's will? Think about that for a moment. It's not a trick question. Who wants to do God's will?"

She stayed quiet.

"God," he replied, catching the edge of what he had missed.

She smiled. "People get scared thinking this is too hard a prayer to tackle, not realizing that it is actually the easiest prayer of them all." She held up her hand and used her fingers to take him through it.

"Someone dies early. Satan has killed a person with disease or other means. It's a situation that is clearly outside of God's will.

"It's God's desire that this person not be dead. The only way they are going to be alive is if God raises them from the dead. So God wants to raise them from the dead.

"Now you enter the picture. It's you and it's God and it's a dead person.

"Who wants this person to be alive? God. And who wants his will to be done on earth? God. The Holy Spirit is God on earth; his name literally means 'one called alongside to help you'. He's with you to do what He Himself, God, wants done.

"So you find the courage to speak and you say, 'God I'd like you to do what you desire to do on earth. I ask you to give this person back his life.' Then you turn to the person and say, 'in Jesus' name, wake up.'

"And the person opens their eyes."

She gave him a moment then smiled. "Listen to it again in slightly different words.

"Someone dies early. It is God's desire that this person not be dead.

"God wants his own will to be done on earth—the Lord's Prayer— 'your kingdom come, your will be done, on earth as it is in heaven.' Jesus has all authority in heaven and on earth. Satan has none. Death has none. Jesus holds the keys of death.

"Now you enter the picture. It's you and it's God and it's a dead person. The Holy Spirit is with you; God isn't off somewhere else, he's literally right there with you.

"Ryan, God desires to do his own will. In this situation, how hard is it going to be for you to have success? God is with you wanting to do what he himself desires, he's just decided to work with you to get it done rather than work independent of you. He's given you the privilege of speaking for him. You have to pray. That's it. If you understand the situation you're in, you can simply turn to the person and say 'in Jesus' name, wake up.'

"Or you can pray with more words, 'God, this person died early. God, this isn't your will, you want this person to be alive. God, do what you want to do on earth. Raise this person from the dead.' and you turn to the person and say, 'In Jesus' name, I now tell you to wake up.'

"A few words or a few sentences, either way, God is raising that person from the dead. They wake up because God wants them to be alive. God wants to answer this prayer.

"We see a resurrection as hard. God sees it as, 'I resurrected my son, now who do you need resurrected? I just need a name.' The Holy Spirit breathes on someone and they are alive again. We do the speaking and say what is going to happen. God does the doing."

Ryan sat forward. He'd seen it now and even more, had heard her confidence. "Connie, how many people have you raised from the dead?"

"More than you, less than George."

He felt himself grinning.

He had one critical question. "Who has died early? How do you define it?"

She laughed. "A good question," she admitted. "I have a few rules of thumb: Any young person. Any mother or father of young children. Anyone who dies before their parents. In Luke 7, the funeral procession, a man has died.

Jesus sees his mother, a widow, in the crowd and Jesus has compassion on her and raises her son from the dead.

"Anyone, of any age, who I think wasn't a Christian and would go to hell if they stayed dead. God's will is that none would perish. I've already got God's word on the fact he doesn't want this person dead under these circumstances. That's the easiest prayer of all. 'Death, in Jesus' name, get your hands off this person.' Then tell the person to wake up.

"Anyone under 120 years old who desires to live a long life on earth. In general, I won't pray to raise a Christian who is 90 years or older unless I know them and they have told me they want to live to 100 or 120; then I'll pray to raise them from the dead. People have a right after a certain age to just let their decision be their own.

"Anyone in those categories dead less than 14 days. God doesn't want people sitting by a grave three months after someone died asking God to bring them back to life. Grieving needs to be allowed to begin and run its course. 14 days is enough for word to arrive that someone has died and for me to travel to where they are if that's necessary. Less than 4 days is putting God in a box smaller than his willingness to act; more than 2 weeks is creating some chaos with the answer and God isn't a God of chaos. I asked for a number and God said 14 days, so that's where my own comfort level rests."

"Why haven't you been doing this quietly around Chicago since you got here? Why haven't you asked a hospital if you could pray for every person when they die before the hospital physician pronounces someone dead and gives an official time of death, before the families are notified of the death?"

She didn't answer him.

And Ryan got his eyes opened. "Oh! You have been."

He ran through the implications of that. "And I'll answer my own next question. It's not your job to pray for every person who dies in the world, or even in the Chicago area. God has a body of believers. God has some he wants you to pray for and others are someone else's responsibility."

Connie nodded. "My way of handling this is mostly learned wisdom. Jesus healed everyone who came to him and everyone his Father sent him to heal. I follow the same model. If you die in my vicinity, I'm going to pray to raise you from the dead. Otherwise, I go where God sends me. God isn't whispering so softly I miss his directions. When God has someone he wants me to pray for, he'll make sure I know the where and when.

"I have a responsibility to train others, to share what I know, just as George taught me and I am doing that with a small group that can put that training to immediate use— paramedics, a surgeon and the like. I didn't choose you, but you managed to nominate yourself. Mostly I'm training the group how to heal the sick, so people get well rather than die. That's actually harder to teach than how to raise the dead."

She shifted back in her seat, sat quietly, gave him time to think about what she'd said. "Ready for the best part?"

He was stunned to realize there was more. "Sure."

"God wants his will to be done on earth. That's actually the secret to everything, Ryan. When you pray for something God wants, who is the one who most desires to answer your prayer? God.

"You may deeply want your prayer answered, but God wants to answer it with a passion to the depth of his being. It's his will, his own desire and he's been longing for you to pray so he can answer you.

"God respects man's free will. God gave us the responsibility to pray. If we pray, God will answer. God will do his own will on earth with joy. If we don't pray, both we and God miss out.

"All the promises God has written in scripture are things he wants to do. They are his desires. We like those promises because they are good things we'll enjoy. But to God, those promises are his personal desires, what God personally wants to do. He's aching for someone to pray and ask him so he can answer. God will not do his will on earth without us. He has committed himself to us being part of the process for how he will rule over the earth. So he longs for people to pray. It gives him joy when he can answer a prayer and deliver one of those promises to earth. We co-labor with God. Want to thrill God's heart? Pray his promises.

For all the promises of God find their Yes in him [Jesus]. That is why we utter the Amen through him, to the glory of God. (2 Corinthians 1:20)

"I've got it, Connie," Ryan said, not finding words to better express what he was feeling, it was so intense.

She smiled. "I know you do; I can see the truth reflecting in your expression."

"I'm sorry I'm out of time. I need to get started on the prep work."

Ryan stood and pushed in his chair. "Connie, it was the best conversation I can remember ever having about God."

"I'm glad you're soaking this stuff in like a sponge. You were ready to hear it, Ryan. That's why it's connecting now. And it's why God rather pushed you onto my calendar." She laughed. "This wasn't at all what I thought the topic should be this morning."

"I want the rest of it, all the lessons you've got to share."

"We'll get to them," Connie agreed.

She walked him to the door, showed him out and locked it behind him.

The rain had paused, the clouds overhead were still gray cast, but it had turned simply windy damp. Ryan looked at the time. 8:45 a.m. She'd managed in under an hour to convince him he could raise the dead and given him the confidence to actually try. He shut off the recording and immediately made a duplicate copy.

"God, there aren't words rich enough for saying this thanks. Wow."

****

Ryan Notes / conversation six / additional references

The reason the Son of God appeared was to destroy the devil's work. (1 John 3:8b NIV)

Then the LORD said, "My Spirit will not contend with humans forever, for they are mortal; their days will be a hundred and twenty years." Genesis 6:3 NIV)

Moses was 120 years old when he died, yet his eyesight was clear and he was as strong as ever. (Deuteronomy 34:7 NLT)

On the day the LORD gave the Amorites over to Israel, Joshua said to the LORD in the presence of Israel: "Sun, stand still over Gibeon and you, moon, over the Valley of Aijalon." So the sun stood still and the moon stopped, till the nation avenged itself on its enemies, as it is written in the Book of Jashar. The sun stopped in the middle of the sky and delayed going down about a full day. There has never been a day like it before or since, a day when the LORD listened to a human being. Surely the LORD was fighting for Israel! (Joshua 10:12-14 NIV)

Elijah was a human being, even as we are. He prayed earnestly that it would not rain and it did not rain on the land for three and a half years. Again he prayed and the heavens gave rain and the earth produced its crops. (James 5:17-18 NIV)

Elisha died and was buried. Now Moabite raiders used to enter the country every spring. Once while some Israelites were burying a man, suddenly they saw a band of raiders; so they threw the man's body into Elisha's tomb. When the body touched Elisha's bones, the man came to life and stood up on his feet. (2 Kings 13:20-21 NIV)

In those days Hezekiah became ill and was at the point of death. Hezekiah turned his face to the wall and prayed to the LORD, "Remember, LORD, how I have walked before you faithfully and with wholehearted devotion and have done what is good in your eyes." And Hezekiah wept bitterly. Before Isaiah had left the middle court, the word of the LORD came to him: "Go back and tell Hezekiah, the ruler of my people, 'This is what the LORD, the God of your father David, says: I have heard your prayer and seen your tears; I will heal you. On the third day from now you will go up to the temple of the LORD. I will add fifteen years to your life." (2 Kings.20:1a,2-6a NIV)

By faith Abraham, when God tested him, offered Isaac as a sacrifice. He who had embraced the promises was about to sacrifice his one and only son, even though God had said to him, "It is through Isaac that your offspring will be reckoned." Abraham reasoned that God could even raise the dead and so in a manner of speaking he did receive Isaac back from death. (Hebrews 11:17-19 NIV)

Abraham offering Isaac as a sacrifice / full passage / Genesis 22:1-18

Children, obey your parents in the Lord, for this is right. "Honor your father and mother" – which is the first commandment with a promise – "so that it may go well with you and that you may enjoy long life on the earth." (Ephesians 6:1-3 NIV)

For to me [Paul], to live is Christ and to die is gain. If I am to go on living in the body, this will mean fruitful labor for me. Yet what shall I choose? I do not know! I am torn between the two: I desire to depart and be with Christ, which is better by far; but it is more necessary for you that I remain in the body. Convinced of this, I know that I will remain and I will continue with all of you for your progress and joy in the faith, so that through my being with you again your boasting in Christ Jesus will abound on account of me. (Philippians 1:21-26 NIV)

Then one of the synagogue leaders, named Jairus, came and when he saw Jesus, he fell at his feet. He pleaded earnestly with him, "My little daughter is dying. Please come and put your hands on her so that she will be healed and live." So Jesus went with him. A large crowd followed and pressed around him. ... some people came from the house of Jairus, the synagogue leader. "Your daughter is dead," they said. "Why bother the teacher anymore?" Overhearing what they said, Jesus told him, "Don't be afraid; just believe." He did not let anyone follow him except Peter, James and John the brother of James. When they came to the home of the synagogue leader, Jesus saw a commotion, with people crying and wailing loudly. He went in and said to them, "Why all this commotion and wailing? The child is not dead but asleep." But they laughed at him. After he put them all out, he took the child's father and mother and the disciples who were with him and went in where the child was. He took her by the hand and said to her, "Talitha koum!" (which means "Little girl, I say to you, get up!"). Immediately the girl stood up and began to walk around (she was twelve years old). At this they were completely astonished. He gave strict orders not to let anyone know about this and told them to give her something to eat. (Mark 5:22-24, 35b-43 NIV)

Soon afterward, Jesus went to a town called Nain and his disciples and a large crowd went along with him. As he approached the town gate, a dead person was being carried out--the only son of his mother and she was a widow. And a large crowd from the town was with her. When the Lord saw her, his heart went out to her and he said, "Don't cry." Then he went up and touched the bier they were carrying him on and the bearers stood still. He said, "Young man, I say to you, get up!" The dead man sat up and began to talk and Jesus gave him back to his mother. They were all filled with awe and praised God. "A great prophet has appeared among us," they said. "God has come to help his people." This news about Jesus spread throughout Judea and the surrounding country. (Luke 7:11-17 NIV)

As Peter traveled about the country, he went to visit the Lord's people who lived in Lydda. There he found a man named Aeneas, who was paralyzed and had been bedridden for eight years. "Aeneas," Peter said to him, "Jesus Christ heals you. Get up and roll up your mat." Immediately Aeneas got up. All those who lived in Lydda and Sharon saw him and turned to the Lord. In Joppa there was a disciple named Tabitha (in Greek her name is Dorcas); she was always doing good and helping the poor. About that time she became sick and died and her body was washed and placed in an upstairs room. Lydda was near Joppa; so when the disciples heard that Peter was in Lydda, they sent two men to him and urged him, "Please come at once!" Peter went with them and when he arrived he was taken upstairs to the room. All the widows stood around him, crying and showing him the robes and other clothing that Dorcas had made while she was still with them. Peter sent them all out of the room; then he got down on his knees and prayed. Turning toward the dead woman, he said, "Tabitha, get up." She opened her eyes and seeing Peter she sat up. He took her by the hand and helped her to her feet. Then he called for the believers, especially the widows and presented her to them alive. This became known all over Joppa and many people believed in the Lord. Peter stayed in Joppa for some time with a tanner named Simon. (Acts 9:32-43 NIV)

****

Ryan chose to start the longer of the audios Connie had given him for the drive home.

"Let's start with a scripture: And he [Jesus] went about all Galilee, teaching in their synagogues and preaching the gospel of the kingdom and healing every disease and every infirmity among the people. (Matthew 4:23)

"That verse is a good summary of the public years of his ministry. Jesus also invested a great deal of his time privately in teaching a group of disciples, 12 men in particular. Jesus is teaching them with the intention that they become like him. 'A disciple is not above his teacher, but every one when he is fully taught will be like his teacher.' (Luke 6:40) There's a day in particular where that training gets very interesting.

And he [Jesus] called the twelve together and gave them power and authority over all demons and to cure diseases and he sent them out to preach the kingdom of God and to heal. (Luke 9:1-2)

"Jesus says it's time to learn by doing. These guys were mostly fishermen, common guys, who at this point were not born-again, who didn't have the Holy Spirit dwelling in them, for that would come only after the resurrection. They were simply guys who had been with Jesus and had been taught by him.

"Jesus gave them power and authority. How did he do that? Jesus gave them what he had. It's Jesus saying to the twelve, 'I'm sharing my authority as a son of God with you and the Holy Spirit that is with me, I'm sending him out to be with you.' Matthew says Jesus sent out the 12 with the instructions to 'heal the sick, raise the dead, cleanse lepers, cast out demons and preach as you go, saying, 'The kingdom of heaven is at hand.''

"The twelve go out and they heal people and cast out demons in Jesus' name. It's a big deal. No one in the history of scripture has ever acted like this group of guys. For the rest of their lives you see people bringing those who are sick to these men expecting them to heal the sick like Jesus does. Jesus has successfully made disciples who do what he does. He's managed to take guys, fishermen mostly, who aren't well-versed in the word of God and turn them into evangelists who can heal people and do it in less than three years. Jesus is a very skilled teacher. What the 12 needed was training, delegated authority and the Holy Spirit and they were able to do miracles. But Jesus isn't finished.

After this the Lord appointed seventy others and sent them on ahead of him, two by two, into every town and place where he himself was about to come. And he said to them, "The harvest is plentiful, but the laborers are few; pray therefore the Lord of the harvest to send out laborers into his harvest. Whenever you enter a town and they receive you, eat what is set before you; heal the sick in it and say to them, 'The kingdom of God has come near to you.' (Luke 10:1-2, 8-9)

"Jesus sends out 70 more disciples, those who haven't been with him as tightly as the 12 have; he sends them out to learn by doing, to heal the sick and preach the kingdom of God and he tells them to start praying for more laborers, because Jesus wants to send more than just the 70 into the harvest. Jesus gives them instructions, delegates authority and he sends the Holy Spirit with them. They come back full of joy. They've healed the sick, preached, even cast out demons in Jesus' name. Jesus has successfully taught a group of 70 to be like him. What it took was training, delegated authority, the Holy Spirit and they were enabled to do miracles. There's a pattern developing here.

The seventy returned with joy, saying, "Lord, even the demons are subject to us in your name!" And he said to them, "I saw Satan fall like lightning from heaven. Behold, I have given you authority to tread upon serpents and scorpions and over all the power of the enemy; and nothing shall hurt you. Nevertheless do not rejoice in this, that the spirits are subject to you; but rejoice that your names are written in heaven." In that same hour he rejoiced in the Holy Spirit and said, "I thank thee, Father, Lord of heaven and earth, that thou hast hidden these things from the wise and understanding and revealed them to babes; yea, Father, for such was thy gracious will. (Luke 10:17-21)

"What had just been revealed to the 70 disciples that has Jesus bursting with joy? It's that, in the kingdom of God, ordinary men would again rule the earth with the power of God, having authority over the devil and demons, over disease and sickness, by the Holy Spirit being with them. The dominion over the earth, given to mankind by God in the garden of Eden, is being returned to mankind by Jesus. Jesus is training his disciples how they will rule over sickness and disease, over demons and all the power of satan, in his name.

"After his resurrection, before Jesus returns to heaven, he spends 40 days talking to his disciples about the kingdom of God and giving them instructions. There's a particular conversation Matthew records that is worth considering in detail.

Now the eleven disciples went to Galilee, to the mountain to which Jesus had directed them. And when they saw him they worshiped him; but some doubted. And Jesus came and said to them, "All authority in heaven and on earth has been given to me. Go therefore and make disciples of all nations, baptizing them in the name of the Father and of the Son and of the Holy Spirit, teaching them to observe all that I have commanded you; and lo, I am with you always, to the close of the age." (Matthew 28:16-20)

"Jesus is talking to the 12 disciples (less Judas) and he's basically saying, the teaching and training I put you guys through, put your disciples through that same training course.

"Observe means to do. Teach them, give instruction, so they know what to do; to observe, to do in like manner, all I have commanded you. What had Jesus commanded the 12 to do? Heal the sick, raise the dead, cleanse lepers, cast out demons and preach the kingdom of God has come.

"The 12 disciples were to teach others, show them how to do stuff, just like Jesus had done with them, until the new disciples looked like the original ones who were teaching them. It's Peter and Paul's instruction to the believers, 'Imitate me as I imitate Christ.'

"The 12 and then the 70 are the early pictures, the examples, of what Jesus was going to bring to life on a larger scale with the church. In Jesus' name, disciples would go throughout the earth healing the sick, preaching the kingdom of God and making more disciples. After the cross, instead of just 70 disciples to send into the harvest, 3,000 would come into the church in a single day, to be trained to be disciples and then sent out into the harvest.

"Jesus' method of making a disciple has not changed in the last 2,000 years, nor has the mission changed. He's going to take ordinary people, he's going to ask them to hang around with him and learn from him, he's going to give them the Holy Spirit and the delegated authority of using his name and then send them out to go heal the sick and proclaim the kingdom of God.

"Jesus is the King of a kingdom. It's the reason why we reign. It's nice to know how he restored the kingdom and defeated satan, but it's not knowledge that you nod at, say 'that's a relief' and then just sit there. It's knowledge that leads you to go do something with Jesus to bring his kingdom all around the earth. We are to use his authority to shut down and stop what satan is doing, just like Jesus did while he was on earth, modeling for us what a son of God does.

You are my friends if you do what I command you. No longer do I call you servants, for the servant does not know what his master is doing; but I have called you friends, for all that I have heard from my Father I have made known to you. You did not choose me, but I chose you and appointed you that you should go and bear fruit and that your fruit should abide; so that whatever you ask the Father in my name, he may give it to you. (John 15:14-16)

"Jesus expected us to be like him, to go and bear fruit. This isn't the fruit of character which Paul talks about, this is the fruit of works that we do in Jesus' name. Jesus spent his entire life doing his Father's will. So if you want to safely be doing the Father's will, simply do what Jesus did. Multiply bread to feed the hungry. Still the storms. Heal the sick. Raise the dead. Open the eyes of the blind. Make the lame walk.

"That's what Peter did; he started doing what Jesus did. He healed the lame man. He healed the sick. He raised the dead. It got to be that he was so aware of the Holy Spirit being with him, that as he walked by, his shadow would heal people. The guy was a gushing river of living water spilling out on anyone near him. Peter was doing the will of God. You want to know what a disciple looks like, Peter is a good place to start.

"Stephen. Full of the Holy Spirit, grace and power. He did great signs and wonders among the people. Philip. He healed people and the entire town rejoiced. Paul gets shipwrecked and then healed everyone on the island who was sick. We need to be less timid about being who we are.

We are Jesus' followers. And when we are well trained by the word, we look and act like the other disciples he trained.

"John says we are to walk as Jesus walked. Paul says imitate me, as I imitate Jesus. That is a serious charge to Christians from two of the major leaders in all of church history, not to mention Jesus' own instructions. We've forgotten that, through the Holy Spirit, they are also speaking to us.

"Jesus has never played favorites. If you want to heal people like Peter did, the Holy Spirit will teach you how. We think this generation can't do what the first century churches did. Who told us that? Satan. We bought a lie, so we sit here with knowledge, but no works. Satan is terrified of us. A Christian who understands his 'in the name of Jesus' authority is the one who can plow through the enemy's camp, stop evil, restore justice and confront head on with what is wrong in the world. Jesus is Victor. We're the generals on a conquered battlefield. It only looks a mess because we haven't stepped in issuing orders to set it right.

"A local church in this generation has the potential to be the most Christ-like group of disciples in any generation, to be the top church as judged by Jesus to have ever existed. The Holy Spirit does not train to a lesser standard today than he did Christians in the first century. Jesus does not lead the church to a lesser standard today than he did in the first century. How much do we as a local church body want to look like Jesus? He's willing to take us there. God wants to do more than we can ever ask or think. It is impossible to set a bar too high.

"Most churches are content to be good according to their generation's standards. Jesus would love a church to say, 'We want to be your best disciples ever. What do we need to do?' And then listen and follow. It's not that Jesus doesn't want to lead everyone to that place, it's that we've become mostly sheep whose love has grown cold, who are content with what we see, comparing ourselves to others around us. No wonder Jesus offered the question—when the Son of man comes, will He find faith on earth?

"Jesus calls us to be his disciples, to never stop pressing forward. You are a light. Choose to shine brightly, which is your reasonable service to God who loves you. Imitate Christ and make disciples around you who also imitate Christ. That's your mission and the mission of the church, until Jesus comes again."

****

Ryan Notes / conversation seven / additional references

A disciple is not above his teacher, nor a servant above his master; it is enough for the disciple to be like his teacher and the servant like his master.
(Matthew 10:24-25a)

And Jesus went about all the cities and villages, teaching in their synagogues and preaching the gospel of the kingdom and healing every disease and every infirmity. When he saw the crowds, he had compassion for them, because they were harassed and helpless, like sheep without a shepherd. Then he said to his disciples, "The harvest is plentiful, but the laborers are few; pray therefore the Lord of the harvest to send out laborers into his harvest." And he called to him his twelve disciples and gave them authority over unclean spirits, to cast them out and to heal every disease and every infirmity. These twelve Jesus sent out, charging them, "Go nowhere among the Gentiles and enter no town of the Samaritans, but go rather to the lost sheep of the house of Israel. And preach as you go, saying, 'The kingdom of heaven is at hand.' Heal the sick, raise the dead, cleanse lepers, cast out demons. You received without paying, give without pay. Take no gold, nor silver, nor copper in your belts, no bag for your journey, nor two tunics, nor sandals, nor a staff; for the laborer deserves his food. And whatever town or village you enter, find out who is worthy in it and stay with him until you depart. As you enter the house, salute it. And if the house is worthy, let your peace come upon it; but if it is not worthy, let your peace return to you. And if any one will not receive you or listen to your words, shake off the dust from your feet as you leave that house or town. Truly, I say to you, it shall be more tolerable on the day of judgment for the land of Sodom and Gomor'rah than for that town. (Matthew 9:35-38, 10:1, 10:5-15)

After this the Lord appointed seventy others and sent them on ahead of him, two by two, into every town and place where he himself was about to come. And he said to them, "The harvest is plentiful, but the laborers are few; pray therefore the Lord of the harvest to send out laborers into his harvest. Go your way; behold, I send you out as lambs in the midst of wolves. Carry no purse, no bag, no sandals; and salute no one on the road. Whatever house you enter, first say, `Peace be to this house!' And if a son of peace is there, your peace shall rest upon him; but if not, it shall return to you. And remain in the same house, eating and drinking what they provide, for the laborer deserves his wages; do not go from house to house. Whenever you enter a town and they receive you, eat what is set before you; heal the sick in it and say to them, `The kingdom of God has come near to you.' But whenever you enter a town and they do not receive you, go into its streets and say, `Even the dust of your town that clings to our feet, we wipe off against you; nevertheless know this, that the kingdom of God has come near.' I tell you, it shall be more tolerable on that day for Sodom than for that town. (Luke 10:1-12)

Be imitators of me [Paul], as I am of Christ. (1 Corinthians 11:1)

he who says he abides in him [Jesus] ought to walk in the same way in which he walked. (1 John 2:6)

What you have learned and received and heard and seen in me [Paul], do; and the God of peace will be with you. (Philippians 4:9)

Remember your leaders, those who spoke to you the word of God; consider the outcome of their life and imitate their faith. (Hebrews 13:7)

For I [Paul] will not venture to speak of anything except what Christ has wrought through me to win obedience from the Gentiles, by word and deed, by the power of signs and wonders, by the power of the Holy Spirit, so that from Jerusalem and as far round as Illyr'icum I have fully preached the gospel of Christ, (Romans 15:18-19)

****

"Ryan, we'll call this short audio A because it is less than a minute and it's three quick observations.

"The most powerful prayer I know? 'God, show me the unbelief in me so I can toss it in the trash! Amen.'

"Number two: Jesus himself was never sick. Jesus never made anyone sick. Jesus never said to someone, 'it's not the Father's will to heal you.' They are three basic reminders sickness isn't from God. They are from satan and death.

"Third one: Jesus trusted God. Even the Pharisees mocking Jesus as he died on the cross understood that about him. 'He trusts in God, let God deliver him now,' not realizing Jesus was showing them he was the savior of the world by the fact he didn't come down from the cross. At the core of this, healing comes from trusting God and acting on that trust. This isn't hard. Just follow Jesus. Let it really sink in that Jesus knew the Father's will about sickness when he went around destroying it, then go do the same. Trust God and do stuff."

****

"Ryan, a brief note on prayer. If you feel like you're having to convince God to answer your prayer, go back to the bible and look to see if what you are asking is what God wants. Ask God, is this your will? First pray until you are clear on what God wants, then pray with confidence knowing God is the one who deeply desires to answer your prayer. God wants to do his own will. He's just been waiting for someone to pray so he can answer. We try to lump the two stages together, to pray with confidence something we're not sure is God's will. Our words don't have much faith and when the prayer isn't answered, we are uncertain why it failed. We didn't have enough faith? It wasn't God's will? And we create all kinds of errors in our thinking, because whatever conclusions we draw, odds are good we will misjudge what actually happened. We create more wrong doctrine out of our experience than any other source.

"Most of the time we perish for lack of knowledge. We didn't know God's heart, thus couldn't figure out his will and then failed at a prayer. It becomes a mess. That's why prayer was designed never to fail. We weren't intended to spend our lives down in the weeds figuring out problems like unanswered prayer. It's an oxymoron, a failed prayer. All the promises of God find their yes in Christ. We need to be better taught who God is, his goodness and how prayer works. We receive what we say with faith. We talk to God. Then we speak to the problem in front of us and tell it in Jesus' name what to do. That combination gets results.

"Look at Jesus. He talked about everything from how to handle your money to what happens when you die, said 'all that I have heard from my Father I have made known to you.' What did Jesus never mention? How to deal with failed prayers. They didn't happen in his life and they aren't intended to happen in the lives of his disciples, either. What Jesus said happened. That's our standard, too."

****

"Today, I just want to make an observation about God."

Ryan, curious where this topic would go, nodded and set his phone to record the conversation as they walked.

"People talk a lot. We're sharing information, sharing perspectives and opinions, we're well meaning about most things we say, but most of what we say and hear, we forget.

"God is different. God does not speak a careless word. He remembers everything he says. Once he's spoken, that's what is. There's a story in the Old Testament that is particularly useful in helping us see this side of God and understand it.

"In Daniel's time, it was a law of the Medes and Persians that no interdict or ordinance of the king could be changed. Even the king couldn't change a decree once he made it.

"King Darius gets talked into signing an interdict, only to find out the order was a trap, designed to send Daniel to the lion's den. The King, in much distress, sets his mind to deliver Daniel; he labors till the sun goes down to rescue him, but can't. He has no choice but to order Daniel thrown into the lion's den.

"God sends his angel to shut the lions' mouths and rescued Daniel. It's a familiar true story, but we often overlook one of the reasons the Holy Spirit had the event written down. God had mercy not just on Daniel, but on King Darius. God reversed the unwise word of a king who could not change his word once it was given.

"God was showing us an example of the problems that could be caused if the king were not perfect in wisdom and knowledge. He'd speak a word that couldn't be changed only to find he really wished he could change it.

"God was giving us an illustration of himself, saying in effect, 'Aren't you glad I'm not like King Darius? Well-meaning, but I get it wrong occasionally?'

"God is a King whose word, once spoken, will never be changed. Even God cannot change the word he speaks. His words are creating and doing what he has spoken. They can't be called back and unspoken.

"I think God knew how powerful that word picture would be once men grasped it. It is a tangible living way to see God's perfection. God is perfect. God never makes a statement that he will labor all night wishing he could change. The words he speaks will last forever. And they are all perfect words.

"Jesus never spoke a careless word. He understood speech as God understands it. Jesus understood he was the son of God and that his words would also be creating and doing things.

"Now consider us Christians. We've been accustomed to speaking whatever we wanted to say and it never had much impact; in fact, our words had so little impact we forgot most of them. But God just changed our nature. God just adopted us as sons. Our words suddenly do have creative power and do accomplish things.

"The most dangerous thing for a Christian to do is talk without realizing there's suddenly a permanent amplifying microphone in front of him and it's both the invisible world and the material tangible world around him which is listening. We say 'its flu season and with my luck I'm going to be one of the first to get it this year' and we wonder how come we get the flu.

"God never speaks a careless word because he understands what his words do in the invisible and visible realms. His words are creating and doing things, they have consequences.

"That reality goes for the sons of God, too. God doesn't say, 'oh she doesn't mean it' and wipe out the effect of my words. When God says there is life and death in the tongue, he is not exaggerating. What we say is what we get, both good and bad. We have a responsibility to understand the power in our words and to stop speaking carelessly. The words of an adopted son of God are creative in their very nature, whether we intend them to be or not. They create darkness as well as light. There is life and death in what we say.

"God does not treat Jesus one way and us another. We are sons of God. Jesus is the first-born and we are adopted, but we are all true sons. That is why Jesus said 'nothing will be impossible to you.' God's creation, this visible world, responds to the words of his sons, just as it does to His words. We need to speak with the wisdom of knowing that what we say can't be called back and changed. It's become active by the fact we spoke it."

She stopped there and Ryan loved the observation. "Thanks, Connie."

"I'm tired. I don't have much profound to offer today."

Ryan laughed. "I enjoyed this one."

15

Tuesday morning arrived with a strong southerly wind bringing in a mild spring day. Ryan decided to ignore the wind and went with an iced coffee again to celebrate. They lingered at the coffee shop until the shared donut holes were finished, then set out on their walk.

"So what's the topic for today?" Ryan asked, curious.

Connie laughed. "I'll be making up for yesterday being a light day by going to the other end of the spectrum. Today is a touchy subject. You'll give me grace on this one and hear me out. The Holy Spirit is going to have to show you I'm right. This one is particularly difficult to get across so I'm understood. If there wasn't a point within this you need to see now, I'd skip this one until you've hung around me for a year."

"I'm intrigued already," Ryan replied, starting a recording. "Try me, Connie. You'll probably be surprised."

"We're about to see." She thought a moment, nodded to herself, then went straight to her point. "My body doesn't go from sick to healed because of my works, any more than my sin nature changed to righteousness because of my effort. People make a mistake when they approach forgiveness of sins as a matter of faith, but the healing of their bodies as a matter of their own works. 'Eat right, exercise properly, see this doctor, take this medication.' They plan their own health regime and govern their lives by those rules they've crafted about how to live. Mostly out of ignorance, they've unintentionally substituted works for faith and as a consequence nullified what Jesus did for them. And then they wonder why they constantly get sick despite what they know about the word of God."

She paused there and Ryan couldn't help but laugh in reply. "Okay, wow. I see why it's a difficult topic to get across so it's understood."

She smiled as she continued, "You're going to have to ask the Holy Spirit to bring this one into sharp clarity so you see its core truth, Ryan. The forgiveness of our sins and the healing of our bodies are both grace gifts. Jesus paid the price for both of them on our behalf. They are his finished works and his gifts to us. Because of that fact, they can be received only by faith. That really stuns people to hear, to realize what is being said in the scriptures.

"Separate the two gifts for a minute. Look at righteousness first, the forgiveness of our sins, which we are more accustomed to thinking about. Israel grew up under the law, trying to keep the rules and they figured out over 1,500 years that no matter how hard they tried they couldn't do it. God wanted his people to realize they were helpless to address sin by their own efforts. He let that period last to the point they were clear on the fact sin had them by the throat and they weren't getting free by their own efforts. Then Jesus came, kept the law and gave them righteousness by grace. He offered an exchange, his righteousness for their sins.

the righteousness based on faith says...the word is near you, on your lips and in your heart...; because, if you confess with your lips that Jesus is Lord and believe in your heart that God raised him from the dead, you will be saved. For man believes with his heart and so is justified and he confesses with his lips and so is saved. The scripture says, "No one who believes in him will be put to shame." For there is no distinction between Jew and Greek; the same Lord is Lord of all and bestows his riches upon all who call upon him. For, "every one who calls upon the name of the Lord will be saved." (Romans 10:6a,8b,9-13)

"The only way to be righteous before God is to accept what Jesus did for you by faith. If you continue to try to add your works to the equation, make it Jesus plus you, it nullifies what Jesus did for you and you don't receive the very righteousness you seek. Israel tripped over this point as they kept trying to add back in the law, their good conduct keeping the rules, to what Jesus only gives by grace. If you believe Jesus and what he did for you as your substitute, you're made righteous. If you keep working to be righteous, you die in your sins. The fact that works and grace don't mix is stark in scriptures:

Gentiles who did not pursue righteousness have attained it, that is, righteousness through faith; but that Israel who pursued the righteousness which is based on law did not succeed in fulfilling that law. Why? Because they did not pursue it through faith, but as if it were based on works. I bear them witness that they have a zeal for God, but it is not enlightened. For, being ignorant of the righteousness that comes from God and seeking to establish their own, they did not submit to God's righteousness. For Christ is the end of the law, that every one who has faith may be justified. (Romans 9:30b-32a, 10:2-4)

"Salvation by faith alone is a well understood fact since the protestant reformation in the 1,500's, when the church returned to the first century understanding of grace. We believe in Jesus and we are made righteous. Salvation is by faith alone, not by our works. So the question arises – do our works change after we believe? Of course. We no longer lie, cheat, steal, murder. Not because we are trying by our works to be righteous, but because we now *are* righteous. Our works change because we are now different people. We have been born again by God and are literally a new creation, a new person.

"A new nature is flowing from the inside, outward. The Holy Spirit is leading us to express who we now are. God crucified our old nature and buried it. Our new nature is like Jesus. We are alive with Christ and we are putting on Christ. Our works (our actions) and our fruit (our character) are both transforming as we walk with the Holy Spirit. God has done this for us by grace. We can never earn righteousness by trying to live right, for all have sinned. Instead, God replaces our failing works, with Jesus' perfect work on our behalf. God gives us righteousness as a gift of grace, through our faith in the payment Jesus made on our behalf."

Connie paused there to let him think about it and Ryan thoughtfully said, "I can already see the parallels you're about to lay out regarding health. There's something rich here."

She smiled as she nodded and quoted, "'By his wounds you have been healed.' Past tense. Jesus did it for us. It's a finished work which is just as complete as the righteousness he gives. Healing is a grace gift that can only be received by faith. Healing is the same as righteousness. If you try to be healed by your own works, you are trying to add to Jesus' works on your behalf and you end up missing out on the very healing that Jesus paid a very high price to be able to give you as a free gift.

"It's so hard to get this point across with the weight it needs to be said and still be fully understood. You have to really hear it and see what the scriptures are presenting, the truth God is laying out that healing is a finished grace gift only received by faith."

Connie paused and shifted focus a bit. "What I'm not saying is that there is something wrong with exercise and eating by thought-out meal plans and the other things we might classify as works related to healing and health.

"When we believe Jesus for righteousness, our new righteous nature changes our character and our actions— where we once were a liar, now we're telling the truth; once filled with pride, we're now humble; the list of changes is endless. Healing is similar. When you receive the grace gift of healing by faith, you're different inside. So how you live life is likely going to be different. The Holy Spirit may have you sleeping more, living with less stress, doing more activities. But it's not those changes that produce our healing. Your Holy Spirit led life is expressing the fact you *are* healed. That's the core truth nearly every Christian misses.

"We see a disease, infirmity, or sickness and start a works program: doctors and pills, a diet and exercise schedule, add a desperate prayer of 'God, heal me!' and rush off to deal with the problem, thinking God will be pleased with our efforts to get healed and live healthy. What God actually wants is for us to lay down our works program and accept grace from his son. Jesus has *already* healed us. It's already done for us. We need to see it in the word and let Jesus give us healing as the gift of grace it is. Our 'good works' of living healthy do not qualify us to be healed. They can in fact be a detriment if we see healing as coming to us because of our works. We are healed by grace alone, by faith in what Jesus did for us.

"A Christian under grace, knowing they are healed as a gift, goes to the doctor and takes the prescribed pills, takes a walk every evening and does both out of obedience to what the Holy Spirit has directed them to do.

"The Christian beside them in the doctor's waiting room has a gym membership, exercises regularly, faithfully takes the pills prescribed, knows God loves them and prays 'Lord, heal me!'

"Only the one living under grace will enjoy God's gift of health. God wants to give it to both of them, but only one is reaching out to take the grace offered.

"It's important to realize that God doesn't answer us based on our need, he answers us based on our faith. It's love on his part to say have faith, for that's how he can impart all the gifts Jesus gave us. Scripture repeatedly says 'we are saved by grace through faith'. It's the one condition God places upon us for how we live as a Christian. I mentioned before that the word saved in the Greek is huge in its meaning—forgiven, delivered, healed, made whole—saved is being restored fully to life. God will let us remain sick until we seek Jesus' grace to be healed and take it. It's mercy on his part. If God left us thinking that works get us healed, we would never get off the treadmill of trying to do for ourselves what he will give us only as a gift.

"There's a parallel happening. Israel lived under the law for 1,500 years trying by works to earn righteousness. God said stop trying and accept what my son did for you by faith. Most of Israel couldn't do it, couldn't leave the law and accept grace and so they missed receiving that righteousness God freely offered. We're doing the same thing regarding being healed. God says stop trying by our own efforts and accept what my son did for you by faith. Yet we rush on with our own works and miss what God is offering. It takes a humble heart to stop our independent actions and say 'God, you're right. Jesus did this for me. Holy Spirit, show me how to be obedient and receive from you being healed.'"

Connie nodded toward the garden park, offering to extend their walk another six minutes and Ryan nodded his thanks, turning that direction.

"We construct these models from the world about health and how you are to eat, exercise, take pills, add vitamins and all the rest, to control and hold off disease. As if we are still mortal men, ignoring God's word that we are a new creation. His word 'by his wounds you have been healed'. And the practical instructions to 'put on Christ' who was never sick a day in his life and who is our model of what it is like to live a spirit-filled life. Galatians 2:20b says 'the life I live in the flesh I live by faith of the son of God, who loved me and gave himself for me.'

"It's become the Christian book aisle—how to diet for God and live by this plan and please God. In ignorance, we accept a Christian version of the world's plan and wonder why it doesn't take us where we want to go.

"The word of God on the topic of health is different than most Christians understand. Once we become Christians, we actually are different people than everyone else walking around this earth. We are very much a new creation. Jesus said if a believer happened to drink something deadly, it would not hurt them. Where is that in the world's scientific literature? Paul got bit by a poisonous snake, shook it off and had no effects. The people who saw it decided he must be a god. They were close in their reasoning, as he was an adopted son of God walking in God given health.

"We live by the world's ideas when it comes to health and live by our own efforts and we wonder why we live sick and aging lives. We expect to have aging bodies because everyone around us does. Have we never read God's word to us, his different thoughts on the matter? God not only says he heals all of our diseases, he also says one of his benefits is that he will renew my youth so I mount up like wings of eagles. We'll be eighty and look forty.

"Most people hear this topic and think, what's the big deal? Okay, I'll pray, aware Jesus paid a price to heal me and take communion with better understanding, I'll go exercise and see the doctor and take the pills prescribed and somewhere in that set of actions I'll get healed. They try to be realistic and just do everything that might work to get the healing they need. Without seeking the Holy Spirit's directions, they decide a course of action and go for what they think needs done. Only that approach is the definition of being double-minded. They try to listen with one ear to the scriptures and with the other ear to what the world has to say about how to deal with this particular disease or illness and do both. They become double-minded, thinking that's a realistic way to handle matters. But works and grace don't overlap.

"What they don't realize is if you revert back to works, trying to earn what God wants to give you as a free gift, you leave grace and you step back into the law and expose yourself again to sin's dominion and with it sickness, disease and death. When you move back to living by your works, Jesus' grace has no effect for you. The very things Jesus defeated for you are ruling you again because of your decision to work for something Jesus finished. Listen to it in scripture:

You are severed from Christ, you who would be justified by the law; you have fallen away from grace. (Galatians 5:4)

For all who rely on works of the law are under a curse; for it is written, "Cursed be every one who does not abide by all things written in the book of the law and do them." (Galatians 3:10)

if it is by grace, it is no longer on the basis of works; otherwise grace would no longer be grace. (Romans 11:6b)

So again I ask, does God give you his Spirit and work miracles among you by the works of the law, or by your believing what you heard? (Galatians 3:5 NIV)

"We nullify the grace of Jesus regarding healing by living like the world does, in a maze of our own effort and works, as if our efforts can heal our bodies any more than our efforts to live moral lives could make us righteous.

With Jesus we have forgiveness of sins and healing of every disease. Without him, we spin our wheels and throw an ever increasing amount of time and money at a string of health problems we will never solve. You will just bounce from one manifestation of disease or sickness to the next.

"There is one way to live healed—have faith in God's word and follow the directions of the Holy Spirit, who is God with you, guiding you directly to what God wants you to do in this situation. Everything else is satan's counterfeit, trying to sell the idea that we don't need God.

"The beautiful thing about God's way – it's a free gift. Having given us his precious son, 'will he not with him freely give us all things?' God is lavishly good. And yet we run around sick, looking to the world for our answers. And worse, saying God's will is for me to be sick or have this injury. We assign to God the darkness the devil created. May God forgive us that error!

"It is God's will for all of us to be healed. Jesus purchased that healing for us and paid a brutally high price to do so. God wants to give it to us. The road to having it runs right through his word. If we come to Jesus with faith and say 'yes, I want it and I'll take it as the free gift it is, not of my own efforts to obtain it,' we are healed. Yet we're scared to accept the gift, for it seems too good to be true; it seems easier and safer to pursue healing by our own efforts. God is grieved by our lack of belief and with reason. God forgives all our sins, heals all our diseases and we don't take the gifts. We'd rather doubt God is that good and continue wandering around sick and infirmed and dying early. It's easier to believe satan's lie, than it is to accept our God is good and his word is true."

They were coming back to the hospital and Connie chose to stop there.

"Okay, that was intense. That second half was like getting blistered by a blast furnace." She had taken him right back to lesson one. God doesn't lie. Yet another major topic was laid on the table and they were out of time. "Thank you, Connie."

"Really?" her skepticism was clear.

Ryan smiled as he closed the recording. "You nailed one truth beautifully. God has a plan for how health and healing is ours. Everything else is satan's counterfeit trying to sell the idea that we don't need God. I'll think about the implications of the rest of what you said, given I do fully understand that."

****

Ryan was leaning against the brick building waiting for Connie that afternoon when she stepped out of Connie's Pizza and turned to lock the door. He couldn't wait for the next morning to hear the rest of this conversation. "Tell me more. Talk to me about the fact we are healthy because we are a new creation."

"Ryan."

"It's too important a thought to have to endure waiting until tomorrow to hear the rest of what you have to say. I know this morning was only a fraction of it. You've obviously taken a lot of flack on this topic and not been believed. I'm listening. So is my phone. I want the rest of the conversation. I may not understand it yet, but I'm not deciding what I think and saying you're wrong until I have heard you and the Holy Spirit has helped me understand what you said. After that I might have an opinion, but I don't have one yet. I'm listening. I'll buy you dinner, run errands for you, whatever buys me some more time today."

She weighed his words and nodded. "Walk me home."

"Thank you." He promptly fell into step beside her.

Connie thought for a moment, then said, "The scripture says forget not all his benefits, the first two being 'who forgives all your sins and heals all your diseases.' They are linked and come to us through the cross. When we live thinking we receive forgiveness by grace and health by works, we end up with forgiveness, but not health and then rather than fix our thinking by renewing our mind with what the scriptures say, we instead start creating our own doctrine to explain why I'm still sick.

"We were never intended to live working to be healthy. We *are* healthy. We are the workmanship of God. We are a new creation. I have come to fullness of life in Christ. The old has passed away, the new has come. Listen to Colossians:

As therefore you received Christ Jesus the Lord, so live in him, rooted and built up in him and established in the faith, just as you were taught, abounding in thanksgiving. For in him the whole fulness of deity dwells bodily and you have come to fulness of life in him, who is the head of all rule and authority. (Colossians 2:6-7,9-10)

"I have come to fullness of life in Christ. There's no sickness in my new nature. And it is God who does this for me. Listen to it in the scriptures:

I have been crucified with Christ; it is no longer I who live, but Christ who lives in me; and the life I now live in the flesh I live by the faith of the Son of God, who loved me and gave himself for me. (Galatians 2:20)

May the God of peace himself sanctify you wholly; and may your spirit and soul and body be kept sound and blameless at the coming of our Lord Jesus Christ. He who calls you is faithful and he will do it. (1 Thessalonians 5:23-24)

"To spend our time and money working to have health, become healthy, stay healthy is to live as the world does, ignoring our new nature, ignoring the fullness of life we have in Christ and the word of God on the subject that says 'by his wounds you have been healed', past tense, it's finished.

"Sin was in our soul—our mind, will and emotions. Sickness was in our bodies, because when sin entered the world and attacked our soul, death came with it and attacked our bodies. The process of death is sickness and disease. For God to deal with sin, but leave untouched sickness and disease, ignores his holiness, his righteousness. Because God has made us righteous, removed our sin, his own righteousness requires him to remove sickness and disease from us at the same time. And we see in the scriptures Jesus did just that at the cross. When he removed our sins, he also healed us.

"Jesus bore our sins on the cross; not only ours, he bore the sins of the whole world. He took our sickness and bore our diseases, not only ours, but those of the whole world. That's the gospel of grace which Isaiah 53 talks about in detail in the Old Testament. It's what Jesus lived. Paul spends his life preaching and writing about that grace. And Peter summarizes it in the New Testament in 1 Peter 2:24. Two things happened on that Friday when Jesus died for us. 'He himself bore our sins in his body on the tree' and 'By his wounds you have been healed.' Both are past tense statements. Both are inclusive of all of mankind. We accept Jesus died for the sins of the whole world, so why is it so hard for us to keep reading the rest of the verse, to see and believe in God's full grace toward us, that he has also healed us? 'By his wounds you have been healed' is a statement of fact that encompasses every person in every generation. Oh, that we would believe God and live healed!

"Every person in this world has been saved; every person in this world has been healed. They may not have accepted the gifts, but God has finished both in advance for everyone. How many people have heard what the word of God says and understand that? Healing is like the lost blessing. We've forgotten what God did for us.

"God won't let you work and obtain by your efforts what he will only give you by a free gift of his grace. Health is not by works, lest any man should boast, the same as forgiveness is not by works, lest any man should boast. Satan convinced us of the lie that health and healing is by our own works and managed to nullify in the church the second of the great blessings Jesus purchased for us. Satan is the deceiver and liar who is robbing us at every turn because we're letting him. The Holy Spirit and the word of God is the route to our freedom. We just have to walk with Him, learning the truth, so Jesus can set us free.

"Jesus was never sick on earth and he's certainly not sick now. We are his body. He is our life. We are not mortal men of dust like everyone else walking around. We are spirit-filled new creations. Our mortal bodies are being constantly filled with life by the Holy Spirit. But if we don't let God's grace work in us, we end up living like unbelievers.

If the Spirit of him who raised Jesus from the dead dwells in you, he who raised Christ Jesus from the dead will give life to your mortal bodies also through his Spirit which dwells in you. (Romans 8:11)

"People will choose the road that leads to destruction by never accepting Jesus, never being saved. Likewise, there are Christians that get forgiveness figured out, who either haven't heard about, or haven't chosen to accept, that Jesus also healed them by grace and so they don't walk in that second blessing of health.

"A different example. We can battle with the sin of pride all we like and it will win every time. Or we can see the reality of our new nature, put on Christ and the next time a thought of pride shows up we respond to it by faith standing on the truth. 'Pride, you were crucified at the cross. God buried my old nature. I don't think that way anymore. I have the mind of Christ. In Jesus name, leave,' and pride, defeated, stops trying to take us out. What we let conquer us will keep coming at us until we put it away as dead, replacing it with the truth. The old nature is gone. The new nature is mine. And that new nature does not have a pride problem. When I believe that, know that and walk in the new nature, I walk in the victory over pride that Jesus won for me.

"It flows that easily, the new nature. I recognize a prideful thought in my mind. I identify the problem by name. 'Oh. Pride. That's you. You died. Goodbye.' And I let the Holy Spirit back up that goodbye with the power of God. I don't change me. God does. The Holy Spirit is helping me notice the old man so I can agree with God he's dead. My part is to consider the old nature dead and buried. I bury it with my words that the Holy Spirit then enforces. I simply agree with the Holy Spirit and yield; I let go of the old man, so the Holy Spirit can enforce its death. Envy. Pride. Impatience. Judging one another. Whatever of the old man wants to show up. The truth works for anything in me that needs to change from the old nature to the new nature.

"My best efforts will not make me less prideful. In fact, by trying to be less prideful, I will become more and more conscious of how prideful I am. You can not get transformation by your own effort. But you can easily transform by simply yielding to what the Holy Spirit wants to do."

She slowed their walk as they turned onto her block.

"It's the same with disease. Disease is part of the old nature. You were under the law of sin and death. You no longer are. Your new nature is under grace. There is no disease in your new nature. The kingdom of God rules your life when you are in Christ.

For sin will have no dominion over you, since you are not under law but under grace. (Romans 6:14)

For the law of the Spirit of life in Christ Jesus has set me free from the law of sin and death. (Romans 8:2)

"We have been *set free* from the law of sin and death. That is the good news we need to hear. So you confront disease. 'Disease, death, you were dealt with at the cross. I am a new creation. I am fully alive in Christ. I am healed. I have God's word on it. God now deals with you and vindicates me. In Jesus' name, get out.' We have a responsibility to know the truth, stand on it, say it to our enemy and yield to the Holy Spirit who enforces that truth. We aren't passive in this matter, but we are trusting children who are to hear what God says, think about it, reach the conclusion 'if God says it's so, it's so,' and rest in that confidence, that faith. And we have to quit acting like it's our job to do his job. Victory is Jesus' role, shattering disease. Our part is knowledge of that victory, a thankful heart.

"We can't be ignorant of the truth and expect to receive what is offered, neither can we, by doing with our own efforts, ever receive it. The reason is a practical one – we can't create healing by our efforts because healing is something which is already done. Healing is a finished work. It was completed in A.D. 33 by Jesus specifically for you. Your healing is like a cake. The cake is baked and out of the oven. If you want it, you ask for it and it is yours. What you don't do is start mixing the batter trying to make the cake over again. Healing is as finished for you as the forgiveness of sins and the gift of righteousness, you simply accept the gifts by faith. Our works and self effort take us the wrong direction, away from receiving God's grace. This is why Paul is constantly asking variations of the question: 'Why do you live as if you still belonged to the world?'

"Listen to the full passage." Connie dug a New Testament out of her back pocket, thumbed through it and stopped to read from Colossians 2:

As therefore you received Christ Jesus the Lord, so live in him, rooted and built up in him and established in the faith, just as you were taught, abounding in thanksgiving. See to it that no one makes a prey of you by philosophy and empty deceit, according to human tradition, according to the elemental spirits of the universe and not according to Christ. For in him the whole fulness of deity dwells bodily and you have come to fulness of life in him, who is the head of all rule and authority. In him also you were circumcised with a circumcision made without hands, by putting off the body of flesh in the circumcision of Christ; and you were buried with him in baptism, in which you were also raised with him through faith in the working of God, who raised him from the dead. And you, who were dead in trespasses and the uncircumcision of your flesh, God made alive together with him, having forgiven us all our trespasses, having canceled the bond which stood against us with its legal demands; this he set aside, nailing it to the cross. He disarmed the principalities and powers and made a public example of them, triumphing over them in him. Therefore let no one pass judgment on you in questions of food and drink or with regard to a festival or a new moon or a sabbath. These are only a shadow of what is to come; but the substance belongs to Christ. Let no one disqualify you, insisting on self-abasement and worship of angels, taking his stand on visions, puffed up without reason by his sensuous mind and not holding fast to the Head, from whom the whole body, nourished and knit together through its joints and ligaments, grows with a growth that is from God. If with Christ you died to the elemental spirits of the universe, why do you live as if you still belonged to the world? Why do you submit to regulations, "Do not handle, Do not taste, Do not touch" (referring to things which all perish as they are used), according to human precepts and doctrines? These have indeed an appearance of wisdom in promoting rigor of devotion and self-abasement and severity to the body, but they are of no value in checking the indulgence of the flesh. (Colossians 2:6-23)

"We either live as who we are, as new creations in Christ and yield to God as he transforms us—I am the workmanship of God—or we live this mishmash of part faith and part works trying to make our lives work by our own efforts. That is the recipe for sickness, discouragement, confusion about God and disappointment with our own efforts to live a Christian life. The real Christian life is what most people miss; it is Christ living in us. Anything that shows up that doesn't match up with Christ, it's the old nature. We just haven't told people 'when the old nature shows up, consider it dead, because it is, toss it in the trash and don't live that way. Instead rejoice that your new nature is like Jesus' and you'll start looking a lot like that new nature.' You put on Christ. He wasn't sick, he never got anxious, was never afraid, he didn't worry about life, he just trusted God and did stuff pleasing to his Father. The Holy Spirit was very comfortable resting upon Jesus. We should be able to say the same about ourselves."

They were at her home. Connie finished the thought as she stopped at the walkway to her front door. "1 Timothy 2:4 says God desires all men to be saved and to come to the knowledge of the truth. We tend to forget that second half of God's desire. We receive forgiveness and stop. For Christians, God's desire is that we come to the knowledge of the truth, that we mature as the Holy Spirit teaches us from the word of God.

"We are content to live with our own ideas and theories. We create our own doctrine out of our experience and shape our religion to be something we approve of and agree with, rather than come to the full knowledge of the truth. Never mind that most of our experience is a mismatch of our old nature we let hang around, fragments of scripture we haven't actually read in context, stuff we think is in the bible that isn't and just plain deceptive conclusions planted by satan who loves to add the word 'if' to what God said. The word of God is uncomfortably different from what most Christians think it is. And it sounds overly harsh when I listen to my own words. I love the church, I love those who are young in Christ and learning, but my spirit stresses when I see us stop short of everything Christ paid such a high price to give us. I want Jesus to get what he paid for and that's people who love him and receive all the gifts he has to offer—all five benefits in their fullness. The church isn't there yet and at times it seems to be asleep. Healing is a huge missed blessing and we seem to be content staying sick, chronically sick and dying early. We have to wake up and at least show the next generation how not to live this way."

She chose to stop there.

"Okay." Ryan let that last point sink in and slowly nodded. "Thanks, Connie."

"I can tell, this one was sort of half way believed and half way wasn't."

"No, it just rattled my thinking quite a bit. That's good. I do get the fact you can't have both 'by his wounds you have been healed', past tense, its finished and a life of present works trying to accomplish the same thing."

"Having a conversation on the way home is not my most eloquent hour. I'll see if I can give you a couple of audios that may help put it in better order, or at least approach it another way."

" I'd appreciate that."

"I can't understand this material for you, that's God's work unpacking scripture and helping you sort out where what I've offered is right. But it has been kind that you've listened without interrupting or protesting where I want to go when it is an unexpected direction like this."

"That would just be rude. I'll repeat again, Connie, there are times you seem to be circling a foreign universe to me, but I'm a smart man who recognizes when truth thumps me. I'll listen and learn and if I would have said something differently, or nuanced it another way, that's simply the Holy Spirit helping me understand the truth he walked you through earlier. You're responsible to teach, as best you know the material. It's my job to be the student, weighing what you say, given the scriptures. A smart man accepts the responsibility to be a good student." He smiled, for Connie feeling off her game was unusual to witness and it told him her fatigue was running deep. "You're free of me now for a time. I'll see you in the morning for coffee."

"Deal," Connie agreed with a smile. She unlocked her front door, stepped inside with a wave goodbye and Ryan turned back to the hospital. He was grateful for the conversation. She had filled out a lot of what she was thinking, even if it wasn't as eloquent as on some days. He listened again to the two conversations on the topic on the walk back to the hospital, fascinated by the subject itself.

16

"Connie." Ryan caught her attention as she entered the coffee shop Wednesday morning, for he was at a back table rather than his usual front one. He had her coffee and sweet roll for her and as she joined him, he set a gold chocolate star beside them. "For wading into a topic you knew would cause a particularly intense reaction."

She smiled, picked up the chocolate, split it in half and then unwrapped the foil. "For listening."

He accepted half with an answering smile. "I spent a fascinating few hours last night thinking about what you said, with Jeff and Walter occasionally joining me for the conversation as their own time permitted. We loved these audios, even as we're still wrestling through their implications."

"I'm glad. I made you two short audios that might help clarify what I wasn't explaining that well yesterday."

He laughed and accepted the flash drive. "All audios gladly accepted. I followed you well enough, Connie, the second and third time through listening to your remarks. It seems strange, how much the world invests in staying healthy and you basically dismissed it all with a wave of your hand as a waste of time. Walk with the spirit, do what he says, take communion with understanding and you'll live healed and healthy and have an abundant life until your final breath on earth," he said, summing up his own conclusion of what she had said.

She nodded. "The gospel is that simple. We just haven't heard it. We've heard satan's work program and bought it, nullifying Jesus' grace gifts to us in the process."

She picked up the coffee and sweet roll and let him hold the door as they stepped outside to begin their walk. "I did have one thought on the way here that might help. So let me try one more way of explaining this."

He nodded and started a recording.

"God has saved you, but until you trust that word, that salvation hasn't become yours. You have to decide Jesus died for your sins and trust him as your Lord. God wants you to be saved. He wants you to believe in Jesus. But God will let you go to hell. It's your decision. God won't override your decision even though he knows you will deeply regret making the one you did if you reject his son. He warns you that once you die, your decision is permanent and you won't be able to change it (although someone else still alive could change your death back to life for you if they bring a resurrection prayer to bear.)

"God has healed you, but until you trust that word, that healing hasn't become yours. You have to decide God's word is true and trust that you are healed. You trust God and then you let him be Lord. God will heal your body because the word of his power accomplishes what it says. The Holy Spirit wrote 'By his wounds, you have been healed' because you have been. Believe that, trust that word and God brings that word to pass, that word has effect in our body.

"When someone asks you how are you, you answer truthfully, 'I've been kind of achy, but God has it handled. He's healed me.' You consider his word over your symptoms. These are the facts, but the facts change. Abraham considered not his body but rather considered God powerfully able to do what he had promised. So you lift your voice and praise God. You thank him for his word. You express an active faith. God's word is settled forever, you can rely upon it.

"You cooperate with the Holy Spirit so your faith remains active and alive; what he tells you to do, that is what you do. What the Holy Spirit asks from someone who first believes in Jesus for salvation is that they express that faith by baptism. With healing, there isn't a one size fits all action the bible gives that expresses our faith. The Holy Spirit will direct what he wants you to do in specific situations. Most of the time it is simply to show your active faith by thanksgiving and praise.

"Praise is the fastest way I know for healing to show up. You can't worship God, come into his presence, stay there for long and not get changed by the encounter. The light of God's presence and darkness are incompatible.

"You are righteous because God made you righteous, then you live out that righteousness; your character and your actions show your new nature. The old nature is in the grave where God put it; your new nature changes who you are as you cooperate with the Holy Spirit and walk with him.

"You are healed because God has healed you, then you live out being healthy for the rest of your life as you obey the Holy Spirit who is flowing that new life into your mortal body. Sickness and disease are your old nature which God has removed from you. You are healthy. There is only one rule again: live in God's grace, walking with the Holy Spirit.

"A fallen man's body has no life source in it and is dying no matter what effort a man makes to stop that process. Death has its grip and is never letting go of a fallen man.

"A Christian has a new life source, the Holy Spirit and a body that is healed, free of death, which will live healthy until the day we take our last breath on earth and next in heaven. Disease does not kill us. God says today is the day you make the transition from one place to another. And even that date is under our considerable influence and choice by prayer.

"We haven't understood God's benefits, so we haven't walked in them. They seem strange; how foreign and beautiful they are, only because we haven't seen them modeled for us by our grandparents, our parents, the church around us, for generations. Had the church of the first century been flourishing for two thousand years, Christians would be astonished today if anyone showed up in their gatherings with even a cold and the person certainly wouldn't leave church still having it. We've forgotten what healing and health look like in God's design for a Christian life. We are a new creation now on earth; it's not something coming to us in heaven after we die. We have been healed and we are healthy; that is our new nature. We don't have that by works. It is a free gift of God's grace, to be fully enjoyed and experienced now.

"We let satan blind us, we bought into his self-works program and now we run around trying to obtain through our works what God has arranged to freely give us only by grace. Our works will not make us or keep us healed and healthy. God's grace will freely do both. We are the losers if we try a life by works. Satan has convinced us that God will not give healing and health as a free gift. And we swallowed that lie. We desperately need a new reformation in the church to slash through the smoke satan has been blowing in our eyes. Jesus lavished healing and life upon us at the cross. We receive that grace gift by faith, not by our works.

"Our new nature is healed, healthy and remains that way as long we obey the voice of the Holy Spirit. Don't let your soul decide your life, what you will eat, drink and do. Ask the Holy Spirit. Then eat, drink and do the activities you desire within his lines. The Holy Spirit is the most practical person I know. He's God. He's perfect. Listen to him, not your mind's idea of how to live life. You're clueless to the real picture most of the time. God is not. And the delightful thing is God makes us healed and healthy primarily so we can enjoy an abundant life full of stuff we like without needing tons of rules on do's and don'ts. There is one rule: 'live in my grace and obey my voice.' From that place go enjoy the life God made for you."

She stopped there and Ryan thoughtfully nodded. She was opening up solid new ground on what it meant to actually live with God abiding in you, keeping you healed and healthy. "Thanks, Connie."

"I'm sorry I'm not finding the right words, Ryan. I understand this topic, but can't do a good job teaching it yet."

"You're doing better than you realize. I can see it. I might not understand it yet, but it's still new ground for me." They were nearing the hospital and Ryan decided wisdom wasn't to hold her up with questions now; he'd have better ones after he'd had more time thinking about this subject. "Same time tomorrow?"

"I'll be there." She turned toward Connie's Pizza with a wave goodbye and headed to work.

****

As Ryan drove across town, he activated Connie's audios to play in sequence.

"Let me try this topic: you can't be healed by your own works, again. Let's start with a core scripture:

For sin will have no dominion over you, since you are not under law but under grace. (Romans 6:14)

"Healing is a finished work of the cross. I am to consider God faithful. My faith lets God manifest my healing and bring it to pass. God can't operate in your life unless you believe his word to you is true. Abraham had to believe God for Isaac to be born. God has given you free will. You have to bring your faith to the equation, but not your works. Healing is received by faith alone.

"God has saved you. You still have to accept salvation by trusting in Jesus' name. God has healed you. You still have to accept his word on that matter is true. Because in his word on that matter is the power to manifest you healed. By his stripes you are healed. Believe that word and that word accomplishes that in your body. Don't believe it's written to you, don't believe it's for you and you won't let the word change your body. God will let you say no. Your doubt can kill God's word and make it null and void to you.

"When this body needs healed, I ask the Holy Spirit how he wants me to express my faith so that I manifest the fact I'm healed. I cooperate with God however he leads. I obey the written word. I take communion and proclaim Jesus death is *for me*, 'by his wounds I am healed', I partake knowing his body was given for my healing and his blood brings me life. I express my authority as a child of God and speak to the symptom and tell it to leave. If the Holy Spirit says, 'make an appointment with the doctor', I make the call. If the Holy Spirit says, 'I've got this covered', I go about my life and the symptoms disappear. I am God's workmanship. I let him do the work and I cooperate with what he's doing.

"Sometimes healing comes by simply going back to the foundational truths and speaking aloud what you know in your heart. 'I'm bought with a price, I belong to Jesus, I present my body as a living sacrifice and all my members I yield to righteousness. God, sanctify me by your word. By Jesus' wounds I have been healed. Thank you Holy Spirit for bringing abundant life into my mortal body. Amen.' In the light of that truth, the symptoms disappear. Disease is darkness and it can't remain in the light. When you turn on a light in a room, it's not like pockets of darkness can take their time leaving. Darkness and light are incompatible and light is much more powerful than darkness.

"God is more powerful than disease. We often make the mistake of thinking unconsciously that the disease we see is more powerful than the God we don't see. The fact God is with us, invisible to our physical eyes, is his gift to us, as he's so bright our physical eyes would be blinded by his presence. God's the powerful one, remember that when you look at a symptom of disease. Tossing disease out of our body is like blowing a bit of lint off his sleeve for God. He is all powerful. Nothing in the universe anywhere is more powerful than God. Seeing his greatness increases our faith which is a good place to begin. Then we speak to the symptom. 'In Jesus' name, I am healed. Get out.' It's amazing what our authority accomplishes when it's the Holy Spirit enforcing what we say by his power."

The first audio finished and the second one started with the sound of a faint radio station playing music in the background as Connie began the recording.

"That first attempt was decent, but I don't think I hit the mark, so here is attempt number two. When we try to live by the law and not sin, thinking that we can earn righteousness by our good works, we become like the Pharisees who failed to obtain what they were trying to earn. We nullify the grace of Jesus in our lives by not stopping our works and coming in simple faith to receive grace.

"When we do the same with health, when we try to live by the law (eat this and not that, exercise, take this medicine, that vitamin) thinking by our works we can make ourselves be healthy, we fail to obtain the very thing we are trying to earn. When we look to our own works first, we nullify the grace of Jesus in our lives. We never receive the free gift Jesus holds out to us—he took away all our sicknesses and diseases and healed us. When we try to be righteous by works, we fail. When we try to be healthy by works, we also fail.

"One person accepts healing as a gift and goes running because they enjoy running. The person running beside them thinks that by running, they will be healthy and wonders why they never are. Two people, same action, only one is receiving health from God. The righteous shall live by faith. We are healed by a gift of grace received by faith.

"If God says 'let's take a walk' I go take a walk and enjoy the time with him. I don't sweat trying to keep track of how many steps I take as if that will make me healthy. God can take care of the details. God whispers 'why don't you go take a nap?' I'm smart enough to say 'okay'. Maturity is letting God with you, the Holy Spirit, the one who knows you best, direct your life. Quit working to be healthy. Accept Jesus' grace and *be* healthy. It's a whole lot easier on your time and money and you actually get what you desire with God's plan. On your own, by your own works, you're going to fail every time.

"I can live righteously without sinning because I have been made righteous as a free gift of God. I can live healed because I have been made healthy as a free gift of God. I have a mind which is at peace, I'm not anxious about anything, because Jesus gives me rest. Life is good. I didn't earn that good life by my works, I received that good life as a gift from God and thus enjoy living it. God's gifts first, then our actions which arise out of his gifts to us.

"We still have mortal bodies, made of dust. God says death is the last enemy to be removed, but for now it has no more sting, it has no ability to bring sickness or disease to us. We are enabled to be fully alive in these mortal bodies. At the moment of death we simply take a last breath on earth and the next breath in heaven, alive in the presence of God. When Jesus comes back, our bodies will cease to be of dust; we will have bodies like Jesus now has, a heavenly body.

"We don't need to get sick in order to die. Look at Moses as the example. Perfect health, climbed a mountain the day he died; he took his last breath on earth and then he was in heaven. God told him that morning today you'll die and be with me. That's the way our last day is supposed to be. It's all good for us who believe.

"There is a difference between being healthy and being sick. There is a difference between bodily training and a healthy body. Muscles respond to use. A guy with a manual labor job is going to have stronger muscles than a guy who works behind a desk and on weekends works around the yard. But a man with normal muscle strength without disease is in line with God's design.

"Work out if you enjoy it. Don't work out to be healthy. You *are* healthy. Enjoy working weights if you like it; otherwise, go pick up your toddler occasionally, carry in groceries, do some yard work – your muscles will get all the activity they need while you live your life. The Holy Spirit can keep your body as God designed it to be, healthy and functioning fine all the days of your life, without you adding your thoughts to how to do it. Simply obey the Holy Spirit's voice and all that you need is covered.

"Jesus got tired after a long day of travel and needed to rest. That is how a healthy body functions because we are designed to rest. Jesus got thirsty, that is also normal health. See with discernment what you are doing and why you are doing it.

"If the Holy Spirit says take a walk, do so. If the Holy Spirit says don't do something, whatever it is, the right answer is to obey that voice. But it is very much the wrong thing to do to decide 'I think the Holy Spirit would like me never to eat sugar' and do that thinking you are pleasing God when he has never mentioned the subject. You can live a life of obedience, or you can live a life making up your own rules. You can't do both. God is perfectly able to get his directions for you to you clearly. He may, in fact, give you some rules and until he changes what he says, stay within them. I personally have learned God rarely has a rule about my body and my health; he instead has a day by day voice.

"Jesus said don't worry about food and drink and clothing. Let God solve those questions. Just hang out with him. If someone shows up with pie, enjoy a slice a pie. If someone asks you to join them for dinner, go enjoy what they've fixed. If you're standing in front of the refrigerator, ask God, is there anything here I should not eat? If you should not have something, he'll tell you. Then within that answer, eat what you enjoy. God is involved in what your days are going to be and knows how they will unfold. Let him handle food and drink and stop stressing about doing it for yourself.

"There will be days you get up and before your feet hit the floor, you'll hear the whisper, 'let's fast today'. The right answer is to say 'okay' and you'll find in that agreement with his word the reality you won't be particularly interested in food that day. Another day, you'll be getting hungry and think 'a hamburger sounds really good right now' and without you planning it you'll find yourself sitting down to a hamburger and fries that night because friends invited you to join them for a casual meal.

"God is a very present interactive God who enjoys living life with us. God made food to be enjoyed. He made doing things to be enjoyed. Don't turn the life God designed to be enjoyed into a works program you have to monitor to decide if you're following the right rules closely enough. One is life walking with the spirit, the other is a self-works program designed to make us think we don't need God.

"The simple fact is God loves us. He healed our bodies and keeps them healthy for us as a gift so we don't have to worry and stress and plan fitness routines and health plans and spend our lives obsessing about how to get healed and be healthy. God gives you both as free gifts, gave them to you in advance, so that picture of trying to do it for yourself wouldn't be your life. He loves us too much to create us as living beings in his image then watch us spend every day of that life trying to stay alive. Life is a gift from God. It's a good life. Our bodies are gifts which he heals and keeps healthy for us so we can go enjoy this life and planet he gave us. He'd love for us to read Psalm 103 and his benefits to us, laugh with joy and with gladness go enjoy all five.

"When you live like the world does, that should be a flashing red danger sign that you have missed what God offered you when he said come follow my son Jesus. The Christian life looks nothing like the world. So look at your life and let it be the mirror. Which are you living in? If it's not the kingdom of God, its time to run back home."

The audio finished. Connie was eloquently dismissing what most people did as being a waste of time. The time and effort spent controlling food and exercise and trying to manage the body was simply a self-effort works program that didn't need God and would inevitably fail, for at its core it was based on a lie satan had sown that had killed the free benefit God was offering.

Ryan thoughtfully closed the audio files. Connie was trying so hard to convey a profound idea. He could hear her struggling to find the eloquence to make it simple to grasp. A week ago the entire topic of healing and health being received as grace gifts had been foreign to him. Now he understood some of the subjects well enough to pick out nuances in how she was presenting the information. That was real progress.

✳✳✳✳

"Ryan, I have two comments for this audio. Not related, but both I think useful to you. Let's start with scripture. There are four wisdom scriptures in particular you should know.

My son, be attentive to my words;
incline your ear to my sayings.
Let them not escape from your sight;
keep them within your heart.
For they are life to him who finds them,
and healing to all his flesh.
(Proverbs 4:20-22)

"The Hebrew word translated 'healing' also translates 'medicine'. The medicine we need to heal our flesh is in the word of God. A thousand years before Jesus, God is already saying look to my word for the life and healing you need. He hasn't changed.

A tranquil mind gives life to the flesh (Proverbs 14:30a)

Pleasant words are like a honeycomb, sweetness to the soul and health to the body. (Proverbs 16:24)

A cheerful heart is a good medicine (Proverbs 17:22a)

"We are a spirit, we have a soul and we inhabit a body. Our heart is like the innermost part of who we are as a person. While our spirit is very different than our body, we live as one being. It's hard to have joy in your spirit and depression in your body. It's hard to have a war going on in your mind and have your body be at rest.

"Life flows from your spirit to your heart, then soul and body. When you focus on removing anxiety in your heart by reading assurances from God in his word, you suddenly realize your mind went calm and your body is relaxed. You weren't focusing there, but the benefits flowed to there. It is easier to calm your spirit and let it flow out to the rest of you, than it is to calm your body hoping to get your spirit to stop being troubled. That's God's intended design. We live from the spirit, outward. Not from outward experience, in.

"My second thought for tonight – God desires us to come to the knowledge of the truth. Not some of the truth, but all of it. To walk in the freedom that comes through his word to us, through Jesus who sets us free.

"A simple example. There are those who say don't eat meat because it isn't healthy for you. In the garden of Eden, Adam and Eve ate fruit from the trees, the animals ate the plants of the field. So since they didn't eat meat, neither should we. It sounds biblical.

"Only they've missed the rest of the story. God told Noah in Genesis 9, 'Every moving thing that lives shall be food for you; and as I gave you the green plants, I give you everything.'

"Can God give his children something harmful? God wasn't talking to mankind in general when he gave this gift, he was talking to Noah, the only righteous man, the only person saved, when God destroyed everyone else on the earth in the flood. The Holy Spirit begins the chapter text by saying 'And God blessed Noah and his sons'. By definition, to give Noah and his family something harmful would be to violate God's goodness and would be cursing them rather than blessing them.

And God blessed Noah and his sons and said to them, "Be fruitful and multiply and fill the earth. The fear of you and the dread of you shall be upon every beast of the earth and upon every bird of the air, upon everything that creeps on the ground and all the fish of the sea; into your hand they are delivered. Every moving thing that lives shall be food for you; and as I gave you the green plants, I give you everything. Only you shall not eat flesh with its life, that is, its blood. (Genesis 9:1-4)

By faith Noah, being warned by God concerning events as yet unseen, took heed and constructed an ark for the saving of his household; by this he condemned the world and became an heir of the righteousness which comes by faith. (Hebrews 11:7)

"Eating meat is fine with God. He gave it to us as a gift to enjoy. You are not healthier if you do not eat meat, nor better off if you do. Enjoy what tastes good to you. All foods are good for you when they are received by prayer with thanksgiving. If your preference is to be a vegetarian, enjoy it and do so giving God glory; if you enjoy eating meat, God is equally blessing you.

"(Paul's discussion in his letters concerning do you or do you not eat meat was dealing with it as a matter of conscience because in first century Roman society the majority of the meat sold in the marketplace had first been offered to idols in the temples of the Roman gods. Christians were concerned not about the health implications of meat, but whether it was okay in God's eyes to eat what had once been offered by others to an idol. Paul said it's fine, you know there is only one true God, but if your brother is weaker in faith and is troubled by it, for his sake, don't eat meat when you're with him.)

"Ryan, the more time I spend with God, the more it seems like the world's wisdom is mostly satan turning on end truth in the bible, trying to get us to go the opposite direction. The actual truth in scriptures reflecting God and his heart toward us is fascinating in its breadth and goodness. We need to listen to God first, so he can show us where the world's ideas are distorting how we think about him and life. There's so much more freedom and answers in what God is offering than we've grasped. We're healed. It's a pure gift. How cool is that? I deeply look forward to the day every Christian knows and shows who they are."

The audio concluded. Ryan thoughtfully marked the audio as one he'd listened to and scanned the collection one last time. He'd finally caught up with Connie and heard everything she had recorded for him.

****

As Connie hadn't already offered a topic, Ryan thought it a useful opportunity to offer one of his own questions as he started the recording for the morning. "I ran into a situation with my honorary grandmother which has me wondering how you handle something. When you are with a person, how do you handle their expectations about how you will pray? Do you explain why you're going to pray as you do, before you do so? And a corollary question. How effective is prayer for someone when you are not with them and they don't know you are praying for them?"

"Good questions," Connie mentioned. She gestured with her coffee. "I have two ways of handling the expectations of someone else. The first that I routinely use, I simply say I'm going to pray for God to heal you. Then I explain I'm going to do so with a prayer of command which an army chaplain taught me. The wording will sound different to you, but it sounds like him and he was a man who got a lot of people healed. Then I keep it direct to what I want done. 'In Jesus' name, death, get your hands off her. Disease, get out. Holy Spirit, fill her body with abundant life. Now be in perfect health, as Jesus heals you. Amen.'

"If I feel like that prayer was accepted, I leave an index card with what I prayed written down for them. And because I know children are particularly good at having faith that what they say is what is going to happen, I'll mention, 'Have your grandson pray this for you when he comes to visit. Boys in particular love giving commands.' That kind of suggestion often gets followed. I've found that family members praying with faith are particularly effective.

"The second method is useful when I'm dealing with the expectations of more than just the person who is sick – they have family and friends present, or I'm in a public setting. I personally find it helpful to pray in Italian. I tell them in English I'm going to pray for God to heal you. Then ask, is it okay if I pray in Italian? I learned English, but when I talk with God I'm better in my other language. Then I pray in Italian. Then I say Amen in English so they can agree with me. I can pray as I would like without them being concerned I didn't pray the way they had been taught. We've agreed I would pray for God to heal them and there is power in that agreement. But they can't disagree with me on the specifics of what I pray and negate my prayer if they don't know how I phrased it."

"That is an elegant way around the problem. I know some French."

"Keep the idea in mind as something useful." Connie drank more of her coffee and then added, "Prayer at a distance works as long as you see them healed and are praying for what they are to become, not praying with sympathy thinking of them as sick. The picture in your mind and your words need to be in agreement when you're praying at a distance. I don't know why, it's just the strongest overlap I've noticed.

"The best outcome is to lay your hand on their arm, or whatever injury is to be healed, pray aloud with authority and receive their echo of your amen. That's checking off every power base you have, the power of agreement, the power of authority, the laying on of hands.

"Laying on hands is particularly effective, because it's showing active faith and is releasing the power in Jesus words recorded in Mark 16, 'these signs will follow those who believe in me, in my name they will lay hands on the sick and they will recover.' Jesus often healed this way, by laying his hands on the sick, so it's an important way God the Holy Spirit likes to work. I don't need to understand why or how to rely on that promise and experience it. My hunch is that something in the sick person is blocking the grace of healing from reaching them, God wants them well and when you lay your hands on them the Holy Spirit can flow grace and healing to them through you. Your touch makes the two of you, in effect, one person. You become like the detour the Holy Spirit can use to get healing to the person in need. Your touch is the contact point God is using to release his power. Similar to when we speak a word of faith, it's God the Holy Spirit releasing power which brings the answer. He just likes to use us, to work through us and with us, so we learn how to bring the kingdom of God to meet needs around us.

"It is reasonable to ask a sick person to move an inch, but not a mile. Starting a conversation about how God heals so they can cooperate with you after someone is sick enough to be in the hospital is like trying to light a candle in a hurricane. So understand where they are and look for a way through the maze to help them. There's a path there somewhere.

"The authority to heal the sick comes from what Jesus did on the cross. That's the good news. The bad news, it's you, it's God and it's a sick person. And a sick person is still thinking, has beliefs, ideas on what is going on, will go on, they have a free will.

"Satan and death have become very skilled at making people sick and keeping them sick. They try to get a patient to want to stay sick, 'my son only visits me because I'm sick, so I guess I'm glad I'm sick', or to make repeated statements of discouragement like 'I'm always sick', 'I'm never going to be well again', 'this body is cursed, everything in it breaks'. That's enough permission for death to flatten a person. They are making agreements that this is who they are. They haven't realized how dark their own language has turned against the idea of them being well again. Those are not throw-away words, they are showing the idea of being permanently sick has settled in their heart and that's what they believe.

"When you desire to heal the sick, you often first have to get a person to agree that they want to be well. It can be expressed in as varied a way as there are individuals, the quip they make, 'I'm ready to never have an aching back again', 'I am going to be so glad to get back home and work out in my flower beds again', to as simple as the remark 'I'm tired of being sick'. But you need that agreement unless they are so sick God will let you simply act in their best interests irrespective of their words.

"You heal the sick by bringing the kingdom of God to bear on the problem, telling sickness to leave in Jesus' name, by telling death to get its hands off this person in Jesus' name. The prayer of faith will heal the sick person. It's the same faith needed to raise someone from the dead. It's standing on the fact God wants this person well and I'm speaking under delegated authority what is going to be done."

Connie nodded toward the garden park and Ryan gladly accepted the additional time for this conversation and turned that direction.

He could see a very practical question to ask given that advice. "I pray for someone whom I have heard is sick. I pray with authority and with faith, in Jesus' name telling death to get his hands off them, for sickness to leave, for their body to be restored to health. While I am praying for them, fifty miles away, they are in the hospital and what they are saying to themselves, their family and friends, is statements like 'I'm going to die', 'this heart condition is killing me', 'I'm never getting out of this hospital'. Who wins?"

Connie nodded, accepting the question, then simply looked at him. "Answer your own question. Who wins?"

"Jesus has healed them at the cross, the health they need is right there waiting for them. I have authority to tell death and sickness to leave in Jesus name. They've decided they are going to die." Ryan winced, seeing the answer. "So they die."

Connie nodded. "Basically. Free will is the trump card every individual plays in this life. God basically says, 'if I won't let my perfect will override a person's free will, I won't let your prayer of faith override it either'. That's the line. But God will use your prayer for the person to send them as many lifelines as necessary to get them to want to be healed and well again, to change their way of thinking.

"Free will moves around, it's malleable, it's not concrete. They can, in the middle of the night, simply get mad at being sick and say to themselves, 'enough of this, I'm fed up with being sick, I want my life back' and your prayer will immediately slam into them like dynamite going off and have a powerful effect because they've come into agreement with you (whether they realized you were praying for them or not).

"A family member or friend visiting them can encourage them by sharing stories of good days and bringing laughter, can spark something in them, so they want to be well again. They have new hope they'll get better and your prayer will immediately set to work helping them. Their situation can be turned around by their decision to live all the way up to the moment they are dead. When they die, their free will stops resisting you, so you can pray to raise them from the dead. That you can do by your own prayer of faith."

"It's easier to pray for someone who has died, than it is to pray for the sick."

Connie nodded emphatically. "Much easier. It's your prayer of faith, God's desire they be alive and a dead person who doesn't get to vote."

Ryan laughed at the way she said it.

Connie smiled. "Praying for someone who died is incredibly easy. It's simply more complicated logistically, because people don't routinely pray for the dead to wake up, so when it happens, family and friends can freak out, whereas people are always praying for the sick, or at least saying 'I'll pray for you'.

"Praying for the sick has become an act of sympathy and politeness because no one expects anything to happen. The thought that a person in a wheelchair will get out of it, not needing it any more, isn't even in the frame of reference of the person praying most of the time. If you say 'I'm going to heal you', that can cause friction. Saying 'I'm going to pray for you', that's viewed as being nice. Society and the church have lost so much of the truth about healing that our very language shows us the grand canyon-sized problem that has developed. We don't expect people to pray for the sick and actually heal the sick. We expect prayer for the sick to be some comforting words and an affirmation that 'you're enduring this sickness with such a good spirit'; at best it's a 'maybe God will help you' hope.

"Praying for the sick is a challenge because people don't expect anything to happen when you pray. They don't expect a broken bone to heal faster. They don't expect to be healed of the pneumonia right then, or cancer. And that is a real problem. People have grown accustomed to having an expectation of disease and how it will progress. Heart disease, arthritis, cancer, you name the condition. It will progressively worsen until it impairs their lives and they will take more pills, face more surgery, more therapy, trying to manage this thing killing them.

"People label themselves with what the doctors have diagnosed. I am a person with heart disease. I am a person with failing kidneys. That's their free will, in part, deciding this is who they are. We lock ourselves into being sick without realizing it. Those are facts, but not who they are. They are a healthy alive person who temporarily has – name the condition – which needs removed. But they have no expectation and no hope that it can be removed, that they can be freed of sickness and actually be 100 percent healed and healthy.

"A person who is alive into their 80s lives 30,000 days. They die on one day at the end of that. While I'd like to simply say I only pray for the dead because it is so much easier, it would mean letting someone deal with sickness and or chronic disease for going on ten to twenty thousand days for the unfortunate ones, before I help set them free.

"Jesus said 'heal the sick' for a reason. You can't avoid this fight. It would be cruel to let someone be sick all their life because it's simply easier to help them after they die.

"I keep it as simple as I can. I try to get verbal agreement they want to be well and then I pray in Italian so they can't contradict me and when their arthritis is healed and their doctor is amazed a chronic condition left, I simply say 'God was really kind, you should thank him' and try to leave it at that.

"Teaching the fact we are healed at the cross, how to live healed, those are separate battles that can't be done at the bedside of someone who is sick. Heal the sick, then when they are well, tell them the good news of the gospel in a more complete way. That seems to be Jesus' model. He'd have days healing everyone who needed healing. Then days he'd spend teaching. Or he'd teach awhile, then heal awhile. Teach and raise hope, then heal and bring relief, then repeat the cycle again."

They had finished a loop of the garden park and were coming back to the hospital. Connie stopped walking, but chose to stay to finish her thought. "Healing the sick is a different battle than raising the dead. It's more complex. You're always working on a continuum, what you understand and believe as the person who is praying, what the person who is sick believes, how the sickness has reached this point, if it's new or chronic, with all the implications of how people have adjusted to live with it.

"Listen to people carefully. Listen for the labels they have given themselves. They will tell you what the fight really is.

"You can heal an atheist who says, 'I deserve to be healed and healthy for the rest of my life' – you can drive a freight train through that agreement and kill cancer in them easily. Your belief in Jesus is enough. Then you tell them it was Jesus who just healed you. They'll be more receptive to hearing the gospel after they are healed.

"You can heal someone who does not believe Jesus heals today if you can get agreement 'I want to be well'. Your belief in healing is enough. The fact they are healed will change their minds about Jesus healing today.

"You can't heal someone who says 'as soon as one thing gets fixed in this body, something else breaks' until you change their heart. You can heal their present symptoms, but they are already telling you the sickness will simply move to the next problem and it will because their free will lets it. We have to learn to resist what the devil is doing to us, to not accept sickness. If you don't think you have an enemy doing this to you, if you don't think you have authority to resist him, you will keep getting run over by him. If your heart says you're defeated, even though the truth is Jesus gives you total victory, you will still be living defeated.

"Someone who sees themselves as chronically sick always will be. Because at the root, they don't have a sickness and disease problem, they have a heart problem. Their heart is poisoning the idea that they can be healed and healthy. Listen to people, to figure out what you are really fighting. Then you can do some good.

"Words tell you what is in someone's heart. Changing their words does not heal them. God heals them. Changing their words starts changing their heart and their free will, so God can help them. 'I want to be well' is a good place to be. They want something good to happen. They are actually saying I want God, who is the one from whom all good things come. They are opening a door for God and thus for you, to help them. You can find agreement with them in those words and bring a powerful prayer because they are no longer blocking God's help. There's a reason the guy who brags 'I'm as healthy as a horse' rarely sees the doctor. He sees himself healthy. He may have a pride problem, but he doesn't have a sickness problem in his heart.

"God hates sickness with a passion. He's already stripped sickness away from the entire world, that's how much he hates it. But we all have free will. All God can do is say, 'I don't lie, I heal all your diseases' and send people to help you who have faith and are willing to pray for you to be healed.

"God knows people are hurting; he doesn't want this, but God has this ability to respect free will that is foreign to us. We flatten anyone who gets in our way on even a minor thing we want to do. God, who wants to give us only good and perfect gifts, stops when a person says 'no, I don't believe you want to do that for me'. God will let someone stop his goodness on the basis of a lie they have believed rather than overrule their free will. It's weird, the way God loves people. He lets us be free. Even when we make decisions like deciding to stay sick."

Ryan laughed at the way she said it.

Connie smiled. "I've got to go, I'm lingering around talking when there is a prep schedule that doesn't give minutes in leeway. But one last, final thought.

"If people come to you wanting to be healed, you can heal them easily. I think that's why Jesus simply modeled that way of healing through the majority of his life. The fact people came to him, or someone brought them to him, said their heart was ready to receive healing and he could heal them. God respects free will. When you go to someone who is sick, that's an act of love, but they are likely not ready to receive healing when you first walk into their room. You have to move them to want healing before you can give them healing. That's why most prayers for the sick don't have an effect. The person praying doesn't expect anything to happen, the person prayed for doesn't expect anything to happen and God honors free will."

Ryan could literally see her debating the minutes on the clock versus one more sentence. "I love this conversation, but go, Connie, we'll talk more later. You're already going to have to run or else deal with being behind when the sign on the door turns to open."

"You're right. I'm going. See you tonight if you can make it."

****

Ryan listened to the short audio Connie had given him as he walked to the coffee shop to meet her Friday morning.

"Our biggest problem is we take our experience and make doctrine out of it. Someone we care about doesn't get well, they die, so it must have been God's will not to heal them. We've now got this nagging layer of our own truth that says God isn't always as good as I would be in his place and that flows along for the rest of our lives as the undercurrent of what we believe about God. If we were God, we would have healed that person. We kill our faith with false beliefs. We nullify the word of God by our doubts and false conclusions.

"If we would quit doing that one thing – letting our experience determine what we believe – we would be able to push through problems with God's help, get them solved and get the results we desired. God's will regarding healing is clearly written in his word. Jesus healed every person who came to him of every disease, showing us the Father's will in action. Jesus paid the price at the cross to heal everyone. We now bring that healing to people by faith.

"When someone isn't healed, something went wrong. We should face that fact, sort out with God what happened and learn from it so it doesn't happen again.

"Faith and doubt exist in every person to some degree. When you want to have a stronger faith, work on removing your doubts. Faith the size of a grain of mustard seed, without doubt overwhelming it, can move a mountain."

It felt very much like a summary audio, Ryan realized. The material was becoming familiar to him. That was a remarkable fact, given where his knowledge base had been two weeks ago when this began. "Thank you, God." It felt really good to be at this place in the learning curve.

****

"I want to talk about rest today and how it relates to how we receive gifts from God," Connie said.

Ryan nodded and settled in to listen, curious to know her thinking about the subject.

"God gives us five benefits as free gifts of his grace through Jesus and they are the definition of good news:

> Bless the LORD, O my soul,
> and forget not all his benefits,
> who forgives all your iniquity,
> who heals all your diseases,
> who redeems your life from the Pit,

who crowns you with steadfast love and mercy,
who satisfies you with good as long as you live
so that your youth is renewed like the eagle's.
(Psalms 103:2-5)

"God wants us to have these benefits. He does not make the process hard or complicated. But it requires a shift in our mindset. From these being things we labor to have to them being something we accept as free gifts of grace. These five benefits come to us by faith, not by our works. God will not let you add your labor to what Jesus has done for you. We receive by faith and we are richly blessed. If we insist on adding our own works, we will not obtain the very thing we desire.

"You can't work to be healed, because you already *are* healed. 'By his wounds you have been healed', past tense, it's a finished work. What you need is not healing, but to show that you *are* healed, to look like who God says you are now.

"When we enter into the finished works of God – he's forgiven all our sins and healed all our diseases, for example – those benefits become ours. The process of entering into God's finished works is described in Hebrews chapters 3 and 4. Listen to some of the scriptures:

his [God's] works were finished from the foundation of the world (Hebrews 4:3b)

there remains a sabbath rest for the people of God; for whoever enters God's rest also ceases from his labors as God did from his. (Hebrews 4:9b-10)

...we who have believed enter that rest (Hebrews 4:3a)

And to whom did he swear that they should never enter his rest, but to those who were disobedient? So we see that they were unable to enter because of unbelief. (Hebrews 3:18-19)

For good news came to us just as to them; but the message which they heard did not benefit them, because it did not meet with faith in the hearers. (Hebrews 4:2)

"For 40 years Israel wandered in the wilderness until the adults in the generation that left Egypt died. God loathed that generation, because they had seen his works, heard his good news about the promised land and they didn't believe him. The good news did not meet with faith, so its benefits couldn't reach them. God had to wait until they all died in their unbelief, then he could take their children into the promised land. (The only two who didn't die from that generation were Caleb and Joshua who had believed the good news.)

"We enter into the five benefits when we enter into God's rest, into God's finished works and we can only enter God's rest if we believe him. We hear the good news. That good news meets faith. That faith brings us into God's rest. We cease our labors as he ceased his. 'Oh, I'm healed, I see that now' and that truth causes us to stop our unnecessary works of self-labor to be healed. We realize we *are* healed as a free gift from God's grace. Our rest is us entering into God's rest. It is us ceasing from our labors just as God did from his. *The truth causes us to rest.* Our labors are no longer necessary. My faith in God's word brings the benefits in that good news to me.

"God desires us to enter his rest. God desires that we cease from our labors as he has done from his. God arranges for us to hear the good news. When that good news meets faith, the benefits become ours. We *enter into* what God has done for us. God's works are finished, that's the beauty of it. It's not God saying 'I will do that for you'. It's God saying 'I have done that for you'. He is resting having finished his labor. When we believe that good news, we enter his rest and we too cease to labor and now rest.

Resting in God's finished work, ceasing our own labor, is evidence of an active faith. You cannot work to receive a grace gift, you must accept it by faith and rest in what God did on your behalf. Your rest is evidence you believe your healing is finished.

"Resting does not mean lack of actions. A living faith is active. You do what God tells you to do. But the actions you do now are coming from obedience to the voice of the Holy Spirit. They are coming from a place of rest. God has healed me. Now I'm stepping into the reality I am healed by obeying God's voice. The resulting actions are not *you* working to be healed. The actions you take are God walking you into what he's done for you.

"It's like following directions to drive to a party. The party is put together by God. You're his guest. You have no work to do for that party as it's in your honor. You simply arrive there and enjoy the party. Your arrival is accomplished by following his directions. You are healed and healthy from an active faith of obedience. You rest and cease your own labors. He directs you into what he's already done for you. Sometimes his direction is 'the party is coming to you, open the door'. You're healed right where you stand when you hear the good news. Sometimes it is an action he wants you to take in faith – 'go tell your friend I healed you'. You obey and your healing appears. Jesus would tell the lepers, 'go show yourself to the priest,' and as they went, they were healed. Jesus would tell a blind man to go wash his eyes in a particular pool and he would come back seeing. Elijah told Nathan the leper, 'go dip in the river Jordan seven times and you'll be healed'. When he did, his leprosy disappeared. Their actions were showing their faith. They followed what God told them and the healing he had given them appeared.

"Actions show your heart. If you have heard the good news, believed it and ceased working to obtain by your own efforts what God has given you, you are resting. Your actions, based on God's directions to you, are coming out of that rest. Rest is not a lack of activity. It is a lack of labor. You are not trying to work to obtain healing, you *are* healed. You are rather walking into the healing which is already done for you. Your actions are your arriving via his directions.

"Or your actions which show your heart will show the converse, they will show your unbelief, as you labor to heal yourself and keep yourself healthy. We hear the good news, we hear the five benefits God gives everyone by grace, but we don't believe it. This is too good news to be true. There's got to be strings attached. It surely must be my efforts involved to be healed. We decide his word must not be true as written. We try to add our works, or add caveats, to qualify it must be people who deserve to be healed of their disease. Those who didn't bring it upon themselves. Those who are living healthy lifestyles now. Take your favorite line of thought. We change what is written to suit our viewpoint. The result is that the good news does not meet with faith and so we don't receive the benefits. The benefits are blocked by our unbelief from reaching us.

"We do not enter into the benefits when we add our own works. Nor do we enter into the benefits when we meet the good news with unbelief. It takes the good news being met with faith to receive the benefits. Otherwise our unbelief blocks the benefits from becoming ours. A corollary to the fact we get what we say is the fact we get what we believe. The benefits are there, the good news is true, but they aren't reaching us because they aren't being met with faith. Faith is like the transport and our unbelief is blowing up the bridge that brings the benefits from the invisible world to the visible one.

"We must enter into God's rest if we wish to walk in the five benefits God has done for us. We must hear the good news and have faith in it. God does not make this hard, but he insists we believe him and his word. These benefits are sitting out there with our name on them, waiting for us. God wants to give us these fabulous free gifts. It's time we realized they are ours only as free gifts of his grace, to be received by faith and follow the simple instructions in Hebrews 3 and 4 so we can walk in these benefits. It's time we let God be this good to us. Our unbelief arises mostly because we can't believe God would be so lavishly good to us. Without effort and without working to earn it, I'm forgiven, I'm healed, I'm redeemed, I'm crowned with love – the five benefits are astonishingly joyful acts of a very good God who loves us.

"Jesus has already purchased these benefits for us at great personal cost. Get rid of unbelief, hardness of heart and our own labors, the problems Hebrews chapters 3 and 4 focused on and we would find ourselves walking freely in all five benefits.

"The five benefits are not ours by works, they are ours by faith. We hear the good news. That good news meets faith. We enter into what God has done for us. As we enter his finished works, we rest, too, we *cease* from our labors to work to earn the benefits and instead we *have* the benefits.

"It really is that simple and that's the problem. People expect the process to be hard. Expect they have to earn what they are being given. Expect they have to perform to deserve what they are being given. God says freely receive from Jesus, that is how you walk in an abundant life. God won't let us work to try to earn these benefits and that drives us crazy. For everyone in our entire life, from family, friends, coworkers, bosses, neighbors, have expected performance from us. God has a different standard. Belief is the action God wants from us for these free gifts of grace, not our labor.

"We need forgiven. We need healed and to be healthy all our lives. We need redeemed. We need loved. We need our youth restored. We should be eager to take God at his word. And yet the very fact God holds out the things we need and says 'please freely accept them from my grace' makes us leery to believe him. We don't believe God is that good. Satan has convinced us his lies about God are more true than God's own word to us. We think healing and ongoing health are by our own efforts. Who taught us that?

Satan. You want to see how deep that lie has gone? Check your own reaction when you read the five benefits. We're still more comfortable thinking wrongly—that healing and health are by our own efforts—even after we read God's word on his benefits to us. We are more comfortable living in the world and believing satan's lies, than we are living in the kingdom of God and believing God's word. And we wonder why we are sick and living stressed lives. The church has a heart problem. We don't believe our own God. And we suffer greatly for it."

It was a fascinating conversation. To work at being healed was to labor to do what Jesus had already done. Healing could not be obtained by works, but could only be received by resting in what Jesus had already done. "Thanks, Connie."

"I keep trying to find the right way to bring the 'how' into focus. I can feel the pull in this material, but I haven't presented it effectively yet."

"I'm finding every attempt useful, it's adding to my thinking and I appreciate that," Ryan reassured.

****

Ryan Notes / conversation nine / additional references

See to it, brothers and sisters, that none of you has a sinful, unbelieving heart that turns away from the living God. But encourage one another daily, as long as it is called "Today," so that none of you may be hardened by sin's deceitfulness. We have come to share in Christ, if indeed we hold our original conviction firmly to the very end. As has just been said: "Today, if you hear his voice, do not harden your hearts as you did in the rebellion." Who were they who heard and rebelled? Were they not all those Moses led out of Egypt? And with whom was he angry for forty years? Was it not with those who sinned, whose bodies perished in the wilderness? And to whom did God swear that they would never enter his rest if not to those who disobeyed? So we see that they were not able to enter, because of their unbelief.

Therefore, since the promise of entering his rest still stands, let us be careful that none of you be found to have fallen short of it. For we also have had the good news proclaimed to us, just as they did; but the message they heard was of no value to them, because they did not share the faith of those who obeyed. Now we who have believed enter that rest, just as God has said, "So I declared on oath in my anger, 'They shall never enter my rest.'" And yet his works have been finished since the creation of the world. For somewhere he has spoken about the seventh day in these words: "On the seventh day God rested from all his works." And again in the passage above he says, "They shall never enter my rest."

Therefore since it still remains for some to enter that rest and since those who formerly had the good news proclaimed to them did not go in because of their disobedience, God again set a certain day, calling it "Today." This he did when a long time later he spoke through David, as in the passage already quoted: "Today, if you hear his voice, do not harden your hearts." For if Joshua had given them rest, God would not have spoken later about another day.

There remains, then, a Sabbath-rest for the people of God; for anyone who enters God's rest also rests from their works, just as God did from his. Let us, therefore, make every effort to enter that rest, so that no one will perish by following their example of disobedience. For the word of God is alive and active. Sharper than any double-edged sword, it penetrates even to dividing soul and spirit, joints and marrow; it judges the thoughts and attitudes of the heart. Nothing in all creation is hidden from God's sight. Everything is uncovered and laid bare before the eyes of him to whom we must give account. (Hebrews 3:12-19, 4:1-13 NIV)

****

Ryan listened to what Connie had recorded late last night, curious what had her attention after such a rich evening.

"Ryan, I've been puzzling around how to explain something profound about health and there is a passage of scripture that came alive tonight that may be as helpful to you as it has been illuminating for me. To set the stage for this conversation, let me go back to a prior one introducing the subject and then give you this scripture and a couple others and talk briefly about it. Here's how I originally set up the subject:

"My body doesn't go from sick to healed because of my works, any more than my sin nature changed to righteousness because of my effort. People make a mistake when they approach forgiveness of sins as a matter of faith, but the healing of their bodies as a matter of their own works. 'Eat right, exercise properly, see this doctor, take this medication.' They plan their own health regime and govern their lives by those rules they've crafted about how to live. Mostly out of ignorance, they've unintentionally substituted works for faith and as a consequence nullified what Jesus did for them. And then they wonder why they constantly get sick despite what they know about the word of God.

"The forgiveness of our sins and the healing of our bodies are both grace gifts. Jesus paid the price for both of them on our behalf. They are his finished works and his gifts to us. Because of that fact, they can be received only by faith. That really stuns people to hear, to realize what is being said in the scriptures."

The replay of the previous audio stopped and Connie's voice returned. "Okay, that's the context for this audio tonight. Let me read you two passages from first Corinthians, a short one and then a longer one on the same topic.

Do you not know that your body is a temple of the Holy Spirit within you, which you have from God? You are not your own; you were bought with a price. So glorify God in your body. (1 Corinthians 6:19-20)

Do you not know that you are God's temple and that God's Spirit dwells in you? If any one destroys God's temple, God will destroy him. For God's temple is holy and that temple you are.

Let no one deceive himself. If any one among you thinks that he is wise in this age, let him become a fool that he may become wise. For the wisdom of this world is folly with God. For it is written, "He catches the wise in their craftiness," and again, "The Lord knows that the thoughts of the wise are futile." So let no one boast of men.

For all things are yours, whether Paul or Apol'los or Cephas or the world or life or death or the present or the future, all are yours; and you are Christ's; and Christ is God's. (1 Corinthians 3:16-23)

"They are wonderful passages, ones that most Christians are familiar with, at least in part. These are the scriptures most often quoted when people teach about taking care of our bodies and why it is so important. Every Christian wants to take care of their body, the temple of God. It's a love thing as well as one of obedience. We deeply desire to obey God's instruction on this matter and not destroy the temple of God. If that wasn't enough motivation, the sharp warning catches our attention, too; the consequences are serious. If anyone destroys God's temple, God will destroy him! No one wants that.

"Don't read the warning in the verse to mean God is going to take an active action to destroy us. The scriptures are clear that Jesus reconciled all of mankind to God with his sacrifice on the cross. There is now peace between God and man. The verse is rather warning us that God will permit something to happen. Something we are doing is bringing on our destruction and God is not stepping in to stop it. The warning reads as 'If any one destroys God's temple, God will permit the destruction to happen.'

"Our bodies are destroyed by sickness, disease, infirmities, until they accumulate to the point we die.

"Most Christians taking this passage seriously implement some kind of plan to keep their bodies sound, fit and healthy. They have some combination of 'eat right, exercise properly, see this doctor, take this medication, take these vitamins' by which they live. It can be elaborate or a few simple rules they live by like, 'I don't eat sugar and nothing fried,' or 'I never miss my daily walk'. It's a plan that fits the best advice from friends, family, trial-and-error and what they've heard the experts say makes a difference.

"It sounds good on the surface, logical. But without intending to do so, we have removed ourselves from under the cover of Jesus' work of grace and taken ourselves back into the law of works, back to our own efforts.

"Satan blinded the eyes of the church and convinced us to read that passage backwards. He sold the church a works program using the world's wisdom. You don't want to destroy the temple of God? Great! Here's a works program using the world's wisdom. Eat this, don't eat that, exercise this way, see these doctors, take these pills. And we bought the lie. And in doing so, we are destroying the temple of God. Rather than live healed and healthy lives until we are around 120 years old, rather than preserve the temple of God and live holy, we instead live sick, chronically sick and die early, desperately trying to do more 'living right', spending money in ever larger amounts trying to get ourselves healed and stay healthy.

"We have allowed sin and death back into our lives and sickness and disease are destroying us. God will not save us from this error. We must repent—repent means to change your thinking, see the truth and go that direction instead—and come back under grace where we are healed and made alive by the grace Jesus offers. God is not destroying us. Our wrong understanding of scripture has rather kept us trapped under the old law of sin and death.

"Take the passage apart into three sections and you'll see it.

Do you not know that you are God's temple and that God's Spirit dwells in you? If any one destroys God's temple, God will destroy him. For God's temple is holy and that temple you are. (1 Corinthians 3:16-17)

"The very next verses are these:

Let no one deceive himself. If any one among you thinks that he is wise in this age, let him become a fool that he may become wise. For the wisdom of this world is folly with God. For it is written, "He catches the wise in their craftiness," and again, "The Lord knows that the thoughts of the wise are futile." So let no one boast of men. (1 Corinthians 3:18-21a)

"Do you see the incredible wisdom of the Holy Spirit in the fact he placed those verses one after the other? We are told to take care of the temple of God, our bodies and in the very next verses warned not to follow the wisdom of the world as how to do so. The wisdom of the world is folly with God. We simply didn't keep reading the passage. We heard 'take care of the temple' and said 'I can do that!' and jumped up with our own conceived plan or plan from some expert for how to do it. We set out to do so by our own efforts, full of enthusiasm and heart for God, but wrong in our thinking, deceiving ourselves. We stopped reading and have paid a massive price for that error.

"The final section says:

For all things are yours, whether Paul or Apol'los or Cephas or the world or life or death or the present or the future, all are yours; and you are Christ's; and Christ is God's. (1 Corinthians 3:21b-23)

"All things are ours. Life. Health. Strong bodies. Good skin. Youth. They are already given things. They belong to us. They are grace gifts from Jesus. The Holy Spirit is with us to give them to us.

"The first section is what to do – take care of the body, the temple of God. The second section is what not to do – don't follow the wisdom of the world. The third section is how to do it – realize all things are yours. You receive them by faith, by simply believing they are yours as a gift from Jesus.

"Healing is a grace gift from Jesus. Believe it is a gift to you and the Holy Spirit changes you to be healed. You cease working by your own efforts, receive grace, believe it and your body will show over time the fact you are healed.

"Let no one boast of men. We run around proud of how healthy we are because we've eaten this way and exercised that way, boasting of our plan and describing it to our friends who seem to be struggling and don't look as healed and healthy as we are, eager to convince everyone they should try it our way. It's an illusion, that health we display. On the outside we look good, while on the inside we are dying, because we are living in our own works, there is no grace-generated life operating in us.

"Healing and health is by grace alone. When we add man's work plan to Jesus' grace, we fail to gain the very thing we desire. We are healed by grace alone. And we stay healthy by grace alone.

"Let no one deceive himself. When we read the scripture incorrectly we deceive ourselves. At this point just about every Christian in the western world has tripped over this passage."

Connie paused the conversation and Ryan heard pages being turned.

"Here's another passage that goes right at this problem.

Do not be deceived; God is not mocked, for whatever a man sows, that he will also reap. For he who sows to his own flesh will from the flesh reap corruption; but he who sows to the Spirit will from the Spirit reap eternal life. (Galatians 6:7-8)

"The common way this is read is that if you eat fried food and junk food and don't exercise you get what you deserve, disease and death. When in fact the verses are saying exactly the opposite. If you sow to the flesh with a works program of your own efforts, a world's wisdom designed list of dos and don'ts, you walk yourself into sickness and disease, you end up destroyed. You are trying to make yourself healed and healthy by your own actions. You are sowing to your flesh, your old nature. You've come back under law and with it sin and death. If you sow to your flesh you get corruption—destruction. If instead you live by faith and grace, walking with the Holy Spirit and obeying his voice, you will get the very life you are seeking.

"Satan goes to the very verses which give us freedom and uses them to put us back into the world, serving the flesh, into a program of our own works. That satan is a very good liar is obvious to anyone who looks at how he functions. The church over the centuries wasn't discerning what satan was doing, didn't reject the error and has let this deception filter into how we think.

"God respects free will so much God will let us deceive ourselves and end up with destruction. That is a profound reality about God. And a painful reality for everyone struggling with a health problem who thought they could be free of it by doing what everyone around them said was the way to solve this problem. Listening to the world rather than only listening to God is what prevents healing from reaching us.

"For those who have given up trying, don't have an exercise routine at the gym, don't try to stay on a diet, those who simply look with grief at their body and sigh over everything wrong in it, but don't come to Jesus, they are also dying under the world's plan and statistically faster than those who try to ward death off by their own efforts. They are dying because they are still living under works, thinking *if they did go* do something, that is how they would get healthy; they've just paused their works program. They are still living a works program and death is still operating in them, even though their work at the moment is to be a couch potato and eat in violation of the 'rules' they have heard are the right and correct way to live. They are dying because they haven't accepted grace.

"They may not have heard grace exists for healing, or they heard and thought 'that can't be for me'. But without expressing faith to accept grace, they are still dying under the law even though they've given up trying to improve themselves. The world's program of works lives in both our actions and in our beliefs. You have to accept Jesus' grace heals you; you have to hear it, believe it and accept it, before you will walk in that health. Inactivity does not heal you of the error of works. An active turn to Jesus for grace is what saves you and heals you. Not inactivity. A sigh, 'Jesus, heal me', from a person who doesn't think healing is something Jesus has done for them, won't give them the results they need. It's faith in the word of God that brings grace. You need to hear the good news, believe healing is for you by grace, accept it and then you will have that healing grace operating in your life. Your body will show itself healed.

"The Holy Spirit is the Spirit of Truth. He will teach us how to read the scriptures as they are written, he will take us to life and freedom, but we have to let him. We have to let God teach us the truth and be willing to believe it.

"The healing and health we want is here, as a free gift of God's grace. That's the beauty of the gospel, Ryan. What we want is right here waiting for us. All things are ours. It simply takes faith in his grace to walk into it.

"You will keep the temple of God in perfect condition if you simply receive all the things that are yours. Healing, health, 120 years of life. God's blessings to you are a free gift. Stop working. Receive grace. And live."

Connie paused again and he could hear pages turning. "Three other useful scriptures:

For those who live according to the flesh set their minds on the things of the flesh, but those who live according to the Spirit set their minds on the things of the Spirit. To set the mind on the flesh is death, but to set the mind on the Spirit is life and peace. ... for if you live according to the flesh you will die, but if by the Spirit you put to death the deeds of the body you will live. For all who are led by the Spirit of God are sons of God. (Romans 8: 5-6, 13-14)

Do you not know that if you yield yourselves to any one as obedient slaves, you are slaves of the one whom you obey, either of sin, which leads to death, or of obedience, which leads to righteousness? (Romans 6:16)

whatever does not proceed from faith is sin. (Romans 14:23b)

Connie paused again, this time for a longer period of time. "Ryan, let me flip to the other side of the coin for a minute. There's something interesting to see. We *are* the temple of the Holy Spirit. The Holy Spirit cares deeply about our body. Corinthians also says, 'The body is meant for the Lord and the Lord for the body.' God designed our bodies, the Holy Spirit is the literal breath of life within us. When we walk with the Holy Spirit having been healed and we're now day-to-day living healthy, what does it look like?

"What the world calls a healthy lifestyle has some truth in it, don't smoke, don't drink alcohol excessively, those are likely to be things the Holy Spirit will also instruct us to avoid. There is a statement David made in the Psalms, 'I will know nothing of evil'. It was how he handled living in the world. He didn't hang around with liars, didn't keep counselors around who disrespected God, didn't permit sinful behaviors to be his lifestyle. That's a good rule of thumb for what to expect the Holy Spirit to also tell us when it comes to how we live in this body. The scriptures pointedly mention a few items, like sexual sins, which are sins against the body. So is there an evil to avoid when it comes to food and drink?

"The Holy Spirit made a point to say that all foods are good and nothing is to be rejected.

The Spirit clearly says that in later times some will abandon the faith and follow deceiving spirits and things taught by demons. Such teachings come through hypocritical liars, whose consciences have been seared as with a hot iron. They forbid people to marry and order them to abstain from certain foods, which God created to be received with thanksgiving by those who believe and who know the truth. For everything God created is good and nothing is to be rejected if it is received with thanksgiving, because it is consecrated by the word of God and prayer. (1 Timothy 4:1-5 NIV)

"If all foods are good as God created them, but then men process the foods a lot, does that make them bad for us? Do we need to care about how processed a food is? How much salt is in it? How much sugar? The surprising answer is no. A healed body isn't bothered by any food, since by definition it isn't sick. We don't need to work to avoid this or that food according to what is in it, have some plan we manage by our own efforts. All foods are yes, unless the Holy Spirit says no. If we're not to eat something, the Holy Spirit will tell us. He is dwelling in us, living through us. Eating what you enjoy and rejecting what doesn't taste good, what you don't want, will actually be you following what the Holy Spirit is creating within you to desire.

"What about eating too much food? Is that something we need to watch? The surprising answer is again no. The Holy Spirit is our self-control. It's one of the facets of his fruit, singular, that marks his presence in our lives. When we walk with the Holy Spirit he's visible in us—love, joy, peace, patience, gentleness, self-control—are showing in our character, not because we're doing anything to bring them out, but because the Holy Spirit is showing himself within us. Self-control over how much we eat is something the Holy Spirit generates within us; it is not our work to measure or control or live according to some number. God is at work within us to will and to want his own good pleasure. We won't want to eat more than God desires as good for us. The Holy Spirit within us will be our self-control. Again, if we're not to eat something, the Holy Spirit will tell us.

Therefore, my beloved, as you have always obeyed, so now, not only as in my presence but much more in my absence, work out your own salvation with fear and trembling; for God is at work in you, both to will and to work for his good pleasure. (Philippians 2:12-13)

"The original Greek translated 'work out your own salvation' can also be translated as 'work your own salvation out' and that gives the richer picture of what is happening. The healed, healthy, new saved nature inside you is working itself outward and changing your actions and words and lifestyle so that people see the new nature that looks like Jesus. You cooperate with that process, that's how you work your own salvation outward. The Holy Spirit is working and we're cooperating with him.

"Last question. What about being a vegetarian or eating only raw foods? Are there healthier styles of living over others? It would seem common sense that if there was something overall about food and drink God wanted us to

follow it would be in the scriptures. But what the Holy
Spirit directed Paul to write is surprisingly opposite what
you would assume.

As for the man who is weak in faith, welcome him,
but not for disputes over opinions. One believes he may eat
anything, while the weak man eats only vegetables. Let not
him who eats despise him who abstains and let not him
who abstains pass judgment on him who eats; for God has
welcomed him. Who are you to pass judgment on the
servant of another? It is before his own master that he
stands or falls. And he will be upheld, for the Master is able
to make him stand. One man esteems one day as better than
another, while another man esteems all days alike. Let
every one be fully convinced in his own mind. He who
observes the day, observes it in honor of the Lord. He also
who eats, eats in honor of the Lord, since he gives thanks to
God; while he who abstains, abstains in honor of the Lord
and gives thanks to God. None of us lives to himself and
none of us dies to himself. If we live, we live to the Lord
and if we die, we die to the Lord; so then, whether we live
or whether we die, we are the Lord's. (Romans 14:1-8)

"A healed body doesn't care which lifestyle you
prefer. Live by grace, honoring God and you'll always be
healthy. Be a vegetarian if you prefer, eat meat if you
prefer, eat only raw foods if you prefer that. They all give
the same result. Healed is healed. Everyone is healed by
grace. How you eat and drink is not going to change the
fact you are healed. While you remain living under grace,
you can't become unhealthy by what you eat or drink. You
live a healthy lifestyle by honoring God and walking with
the Holy Spirit. The expression of that life as it pertains to
food and drink will be as varied as there are individuals.

"The verses rather show us how to handle this liberty.
Don't judge someone else's choices regarding food and
drink, thinking your choices are better than theirs, for by
doing so you will grieve the Holy Spirit. Call living by

works for what it is, a sin, but recognize living by grace for what it is, too. Living by grace, healed by grace alone, will be displayed in lifestyles of infinite variations, which are all pleasing to God.

do not grieve the Holy Spirit of God, in whom you were sealed for the day of redemption. (Ephesians 4:30b)

No one born of God commits sin; for God's nature abides in him and he cannot sin because he is born of God. (1 John 3:9)

"We will not sin regarding food and drink if we walk with the Holy Spirit. That's the best news there is in the scriptures and a very comforting truth we can lean against as we sort out our day-to-day walk. The Holy Spirit in us will be leading us in every aspect of our lifestyle to please God, prompting us from within. We are to live in simple obedience to what He says for us to do, when He tells us to do it. We relax, stop our own efforts and let God lead."

Connie paused and then turned the subject slightly. "How can you tell the difference between the person living under works and one living under grace? How can you tell the difference between the person eating a salad because it is their own works program and the one who is eating the salad because the Holy Spirit mentioned have that for lunch? You can't in the short term. You can in the long term. Those sowing to the flesh, living by their own efforts, reap corruption, they get sick and eventually die. Those sowing to the spirit reap from the spirit life. God can see the difference between the two, between the person living under the law and the person living under grace.

"The majority of us have spent our lives living in a mix of our own works and grace. That's what the Holy Spirit most wants to free us from doing. You can't tell where someone is on that spectrum, are they living under law, under a mix, or under only grace, based on an external fact. It's more the direction they are moving that shows the difference. Someone who has been ill a long time, finding grace, gets healed and healthy. Someone under the law looks good for a while as their own efforts yield temporary fruit, but their fruit doesn't last.

"Satan took healing out of the church by convincing the church healings had ended in the first century, then by spreading the thought that sickness comes from God, so if you're sick, blame God. We bought those lies. We lost the truth that sickness, disease and death, are the works of the devil. Then satan convinced the church to accept their own efforts over God's grace for how to get healed and live healthy. Satan's play is readable now, looking back, but it has had time to do enormous damage. Millions of Christians have died early from sickness and disease because satan is a good liar and we didn't read the word of God as it was written, didn't follow the road it presents to grace alone.

"We need to fall in love with the scriptures and the Holy Spirit and let him fix our thinking and our hearts. Only one of us can work in my life; it will be me, or it will be God. My way leads to death, his way leads to abundant life.

"By Jesus' grace to me, I am loved. I am righteous. I am healed. I am rich. I am delivered. I am made whole. He has saved me completely. I am a new creation. I see that truth, I believe God, I rest. I cease from all my own works. These are finished gifts to me and I accept them. As I rest, who I now am, a new creation, comes to the surface for all to see as the Holy Spirit does his work in me. God manifests who I now am. It's a God thing. It isn't my efforts. The Holy Spirit dwelling in me transforms me by his own power. That's grace.

"I am the bride of Christ. Someone so lovely of character and actions, adorned in such beauty, I am worthy of the bridegroom, the first-born son of Almighty God. God has chosen to make me that bride. And I've decided I'm going to let him do so."

Connie paused again. "It is now more than just late, so I'll close the audio here. I thought this passage helpful enough it deserved a late night audio; I just somehow managed to make two other long stops along the way. I hope it helps."

Ryan let the recording end and didn't take the ear buds out, simply kept walking. Amazing. Connie had been looking for the way to show him what she understood and she'd just found it.

****

Conclusion

Thank you for taking this journey with me through the scriptures. It's my hope you've been able to see the topics of healing and grace in a richer way and have received from Jesus what you are seeking for yourself and those you love. The full presentation of these truths in story format can be found in the book *An Unfinished Death* by Dee Henderson. The information presented here comes alive when you see Ryan and Connie living what is discussed. For details about that book, as well as others I have written, visit www.DeeHenderson.com.

Further Study

For further study on these subjects I highly recommend books by Derek Prince, Randy Clark, Bill Johnson, Andrew Wommack, Reinhard Bonnke, Watchman Nee, Joseph Prince, Robert Morris, Creflo Dollar, and others, on the topics of grace, healing, and the Holy Spirit. Randy Clark's DVDs on healing are very practical resources. I also highly recommend the deluxe edition DVDs by Darren Wilson, *Furious Love, Father of Lights, Finger of God, Holy Ghost,* and *Holy Ghost Reborn,* (the deluxe editions have full interviews included in the extra DVD's, beyond the excerpts in the movies.)

Author Biography

Dee Henderson is the author of numerous novels, including *Taken, Undetected, Unspoken, Full Disclosure*, and the acclaimed O'MALLEY series. Several titles have appeared on the USA Today Bestseller list; *Full Disclosure* has also appeared on the New York Times Bestseller list. Her books have won or been nominated for several industry awards, such as the RITA Award, the Christy Award, and the ECPA Gold Medallion. For more information, visit www.DeeHenderson.com

Dee Henderson
P.O. Box 13086
Springfield, IL 62791

dee@deehenderson.com
www.deehenderson.com

Books by Dee Henderson

The O'Malley Series
The Negotiator – Kate and Dave
The Guardian – Shari and Marcus
The Truth Seeker – Lisa and Quinn
The Protector – Cassie and Jack
The Healer – Rachel and Cole
The Rescuer – Meghan and Stephen
Danger in the Shadows (prequel - Dave's story)
Jennifer: An O'Malley Love Story (prequel - Jennifer's
back story)

Full Disclosure – Ann and Paul Falcon
Unspoken – Charlotte and Bryce Bishop
Undetected – Gina and Mark Bishop
Taken – Shannon and Matthew Dane

Evie Blackwell Stories
Traces of Guilt
Threads of Suspicion

Military Stories
True Devotion
True Valor
True Honor

Various Other Titles
Kidnapped
The Witness
Before I Wake
The Marriage Wish
God's Gift

Books by Dee Henderson (continued)

<u>Short Stories</u>
"Missing" in anthology Sins of the Past
"Betrayed" in anthology [yet to be titled] (coming in 2018)

<u>Companion Books (read one or the other)</u>
Healing is by Grace Alone (non-fiction)
An Unfinished Death (fiction)

Visit the website www.DeeHenderson.com for additional book details.

51574800R00094

Made in the USA
Lexington, KY
04 September 2019